No Red Meat

Brenda Shriver   **&**   Angela Shriver

RUNNING PRESS
PHILADELPHIA · LONDON

9 8 7 6 5 4 3 2 1
Digit on the right indicates the number of this printing

Library of Congress Control Number: 2008943527

ISBN: 978-0-7624-3553-1

Cover design by Bill Jones
Interior design by Maria Taffera Lewis, Blue Studio Design
Illustrations by Keith Bishop, Pitch Graphics
Edited by Geoffrey Stone
Typography:Boton and Grotesque

Running Press Book Publishers
2300 Chestnut Street
Philadelphia, PA 19103-4371
Visit us on the web!
www.runningpresscooks.com

To Our Family

My Greatest Blessing

Acknowledgements

To Angela Shriver, my daughter-in-law and my coauthor, a special thank you for providing all the nutritional information in this book and for your support and faith.

I wish to thank the people who have shared their recipes with me. In addition, thanks to Sally Schaper, who furnished helpful editorial comment and suggestion, and my friends who supported me with their love and prayers.

I am grateful to my family for their moral support, suggestions, and patience over the years as I was developing these recipes. A special thanks to my son, John, III, for overwhelming patience in helping me with the complexities of our computer. I am also thankful to my daughter, Audrey, for her encouragement and suggestions in developing new recipes. And finally, I am most grateful to my husband, John, my most vocal critic and strongest supporter.

— *Brenda Shriver*

Contents

This Book is for you!

I **originally wrote this cookbook for** people with coronary heart disease (CHD) and their family members who are at high risk of developing this disease. However, through the years I have found another segment of the population, the people who simply want to eat healthily, who love this cookbook.

Twenty-six years ago we learned my husband, John, had CHD. At that time his cardiologist told him to change his eating habits to a low-fat, low-cholesterol, no-red-meat diet and continue his vigorous exercise program.

I acquired what few "heart cookbooks" that were available and started a new way of cooking for our family. After many disappointments, our family agreed most of the recipes were not very tasty and they were either too strict or not strict enough. Plus, we missed some of our family favorites. I began to experiment by preparing new dishes for the family; if the dish got a thumb down, I would make some changes until we agreed the food was tasty and a keeper. Many of the recipes I created by adapting and converting old and new recipes, other recipes are my own creation.

Eventually people started asking for my recipes. I was always happy to share recipes, but there was one major problem—all the new recipes were in my head! So it was back to the kitchen. This time I was armed with pen and paper, measuring, cooking, and writing as I worked. I had more recipes than I realized, so at the urging of family and friends, I wrote this cookbook. Now after twenty years I have revised the book to include new ingredients and also many new recipes, which I think you will be pleased with.

Over the years I've noticed friends and family members with CHD who have failed to adhere to their medically restricted diet. At first I couldn't understand why they failed, but after our family's experience I began to see the difficulty of following this style of eating. Some of the friends would try heart-healthy cookbooks; sometimes it was good some times not so good. There are many kinds of "heart cookbooks"—the cookbook for a more sophisticated palate and on the other hand there are cookbooks so very strict I can't imagine anyone continuing to eat that way for a lifetime. My *No Red Meat* cookbook and the way of eating I encourage is not a diet but a lifetime way of eating. I talked to many people about "heart diets." In the beginning they were enthusiastic about trying new recipes, especially the more sophisticated or trendy ones. Eventually, after a few weeks of eating food with unfamiliar ingredients the novelty soon wore off and they were back to their old way of eating. People who chose the stricter recipes soon became bored

with food that had little taste, didn't satisfy, or was very expensive. They too gradually returned to their old eating habits.

The recipes in this cookbook will satisfy most people who are interested in eating healthier foods. The recipes also include many familiar dishes like "Mom used to make."

In *No Red Meat*, I've included:

+ Vital nutritional information with each recipe.
+ List of herbs and spices, with suggested uses.
+ Menu suggestions.
+ Helpful hints preceding each section.
+ A wide variety of recipes:
  Normal food for everyday.
  Special food for entertaining or special occasions.
  Traditional food for holidays.

In this collection, I have created healthy, low-fat, low-cholesterol recipes every family member can enjoy. Some are simple enough for the beginning cook. Others are a little more complicated for the more experienced cook who likes to spend time in meal preparation. Many are my family's old favorites that I have converted without sacrificing the good taste.

These recipes were created specifically for my husband's diet. While his sodium intake is not restricted, I use very little salt in my cooking. When using certain canned foods I rely on the sodium included but in other recipes I will call for a small amount of salt. If you are on a salt-restricted diet, make the substitutions I've suggested using your own ideas or salt-free products to avoid consuming too much sodium. Remember, herbs and spices can add tremendously to a dish.

My husband does not have a weight problem, so he is permitted some sugar. Our family is fond of desserts, so there is an extensive selection of desserts included here. As I plan our daily meals I take into consideration what we have had earlier in the day or will consume later. If the entrée contains more fat than usual, I am careful with the remainder of the meal. I make sure other dishes are lower that usual in fat or cholesterol. The same is true for desserts. If the dessert has more fat than usual, I plan a fish or vegetarian entrée, keeping in mind the total fat intake for the day.

Meal planning is not hard it just requires a little extra time and effort to maintain a healthy, satisfying diet, but it is possible. Once you become familiar with shopping for the healthier products and using these recipes, it will become second nature.

There are a few products in these recipes I would like to explain.

Margarine: When a recipe calls for butter or margarine it is up to you which you prefer to use. Since they both have the same amount of fat, the difference being that butter is all natural but has saturated fat while stick margarine has hydrogenated shortening. In some recipes you can substitute either canola oil or olive oil. For example when a recipe calls for a bread crumb topping with melted margarine drizzled over all. I spray the breadcrumbs with a vegetable spray and omit the melted margarine.

However, I have found in baking I prefer either stick margarine or butter unless the recipe specifically calls for vegetable oil. I especially like to use butter when a dessert recipe calls for a crumb topping. Margarine is fine to use but I personally think butter gives it a richer taste. Also, in some of the recipes where you pour melted butter over the top, I use butter again because I think it enhances the flavor of the dish. In all my recipes I have slightly reduced the amount of fat and in any recipe I use all types of fat sparingly. You can use this little hint in many ways when cooking.

Liquid shortening/fat: I prefer canola oil and extra-virgin olive oil.

Sweeteners: When using sweeteners, I prefer Stevia simply because it is a natural sweetener and has not been chemically changed. However, some of the packaged artificial sweeteners are better to cook with.

Whole wheat: I recommend using whole wheat products, i.e. breads, pasta, rice. However, if you are baking from scratch I would suggest using at least ¾ white flour with ¼ whole wheat flour. White whole wheat flour is available in some markets but not all; it can be fun to just experiment with it while baking to see what the results will be.

Hints: Sprinkle a little chopped walnuts or almonds over your salad, dessert, etc. for additional fiber and healthy fats.

✦ Blueberries, strawberries, blackberries, raspberries are great sources of fiber, try tossing a few on your salad or cereal.

✦ It is amazing what a sprinkling of fresh herbs can do to an otherwise neutral dish; refer to the Herbs and Spices section in this book.

It is my hope that by sharing my recipes and ideas with you, whether on a medically restricted diet or simply desiring to eat healthy, you will realize food can be delicious as well as healthy. Have fun cooking—it can be so rewarding.

—Brenda Shriver

Heart Healthy Choices

Heart disease is a major health issue in the United States. In fact, heart disease is the leading cause of death in the U.S., according to the Centers for Disease Control. The major risk factors are smoking, obesity, high blood pressure, physical inactivity, diabetes, and a family history of heart disease. The good news is that heart disease is largely preventable through positive lifestyle changes, sometimes in conjunction with medication.

You can choose a heart healthy lifestyle to reduce your risk of disease and manage your health. This cookbook can help you. Part of this lifestyle includes changing the way you eat. Eating for good health will require determination and effort, but the rewards will pay off in the long run. It has for Brenda's family!

Reducing total fat intake, choosing the right types of fats, and eating a wide variety of whole grains, fruits, and vegetables are all steps you can take towards heart health. Below are some general recommendations regarding dietary intake and practical steps to incorporate into your lifestyle. This cookbook can help you stay within those guidelines.

Most all of the main dish recipes in *No Red Meat* have 10 grams or less fat per serving and contribute less than 30 percent of the total calories per serving. Use the low fat recipes in *No Red Meat* as a part of your new way of eating.

Current Dietary Guidelines for Americans recommend limiting total fat intake to between 20 and 35 percent of our total calories. For example, if you follow a 2,000-calorie diet, then you should consume no more than 400 to 700 kcal (calories) from fat each day. To determine your daily fat intake in grams, simply divide 400 and 700 by 9 to get approximately 44 to 78 grams. (One gram of fat equals 9 kcal.)

✦ Additionally, Americans should consume less than 300 mg/day of cholesterol.

✦ To calculate your caloric needs, based on height/weight and activity level, visit *www.mypyramid.gov.* Click on MyPyramidPlan.

Here are three steps to reduce your total fat and cholesterol intake:

Step 1: Choose lean

✦ Select fish and poultry (breast meat) more often. If you choose to eat red meat, look for the words loin, round, or flank.

✦ Trim excess fats from meats before cooking. Remove skin from poultry before or after cooking.

✦ Reduce the amount of meat in your meal: Try a meatless entrée featuring vegetables or beans. (See Vegetarian Lasagna, page 193, and Lentil Soup, page 59.)

✦ Use meat more sparingly for flavor, rather than as the main ingredient, as in stews, soups, and spaghetti. (See Chicken Corn Chowder, page 52, and Chicken Tetrazzini, page 144.)

✦ Choose reduced-fat dairy products made with skim or 1% milk. Use reduced-fat cheeses. Grate cheese to use less or choose sharp flavored cheeses (feta, sharp cheddar, asiago, blue cheese) to use less.

Step 2: Cook lean

✦ Bake, broil, braise, grill, poach, microwave, stir-fry, steam, or boil rather than deep fry.

✦ Use cooking sprays and nonstick pans to replace or reduce the amount of oil needed for sautéing or stir-frying.

✦ Make gravies with fat-free broth, evaporated skim milk, or fat-free half-and-half, and cornstarch.

Step 3: Season lean

✦ Season vegetables with herbs and spices, broth, or bouillon cubes rather than butter, bacon, ham hocks, or salt pork.

✦ Cook onions, green pepper, and other vegetables in a little broth instead of sautéing them in fat. Add garlic powder and onion powder to enhance flavor.

✦ Use soft tub margarine or margarine pump sprays or granules to season foods.

✦ Add sharp, strong flavors to recipes: red bell pepper, red onion, sun-dried tomatoes, cilantro, garlic, salsa, cumin, red pepper flakes, soy sauce, Tabasco, balsamic vinegar, etc.

✦ It's important to understand that the types of fats we choose are just as important as the amount of fats we consume. Thinking of fats as either "more desirable" or "less desirable" can make it easier to make heart healthy choices.

✦ The more desirable fats, those benefiting health, are the polyunsaturated and monoun-saturated fats. These supply the body with en-ergy, help the body absorb fat-soluble vitamins, and provide essential fatty acids such as omega-3 polyunsaturated fat and omega-6 polyunsaturated fat. These fats are found in vegetable oils such as olive, canola, sunflower, and soybean and in foods such as fish and nuts. Substituting monounsaturated fats for satu-rated fat reduces risk for heart disease. In addi-tion, consuming omega-3 polyunsaturated fats from fatty fish (such as salmon, white albacore tuna, and rainbow trout) or using moderate amounts of vegetable oils like canola, olive, walnut, or flaxseed may also help reduce the risk of heart disease. The American Heart Association recommends eating fatty fish twice per week.

✦ The "less desirable" fats, on the other hand, are saturated fat and trans fat. Saturated fat, the fats found in animal products (meat, poultry, and dairy) and coconut and palm oils, can raise LDL (low-density lipoprotein) or "bad" cholesterol levels. The Dietary Guidelines recommend that Americans limit their saturated fat intake to below 10 percent of total caloric intake. For adults with elevated LDL cholesterol, a reduc-tion of saturated fat to 7 percent of calories is recommended.

✦ Trans fats, which "behave" like saturated fats, are created through a manufacturing process that turns liquid oils into solid fat. The main sources of trans fat in the U.S. diet are from partially hydrogenated (hardened) oils found in foods such as cookies, crackers, pastries, frostings, and other commercially packaged foods. Fortunately, the Nutrition Facts panel on food labels now lists the amount of trans fat.

Here are three steps to reduce your intake of the "less desirable" saturated and trans fats:

Step 1: Reduce your total fat intake.

✦ See the above steps. By following these steps you are also reducing your saturated fat intake!

Step 2: Replace "less desirable" fats with "more desirable" fats.

✦ Replace butter, lard, shortening, and hard stick margarine with unsaturated fats such as soft, nonhydrogenated margarine and vegetable oils like olive or canola oil whenever possible. Reserve baked goods made with "less desirable" fats for special occasions and consume in moderation.

✦ In cheese sauces, use fat-free milk and reduced fat cheese instead of whole milk, regular cheese, and butter. Also, use evaporated skim milk or fat-free half-and-half, replacing whole milk or cream. (Try Macaroni and Cheese, page 191.)

✦ When sautéing, for example, instead of using 1 tablespoon butter, try using 2 tablespoons broth or wine, or 1 teaspoon olive oil with vegetable cooking spray and a nonstick pan, or tub margarine.

✦ Try replacing one entrée per week with fatty fish. Move toward a goal of twice per week. (See Grilled Salmon, page 182.)

Step 3: Read the Nutrition Facts panel to make wise choices.

✦ Look for foods that are low in saturated and trans fat. Saturated and trans fats should total less than 3 grams per serving.

✦ Compare similar foods to find out which one is lower in fat.

✦ Be mindful of the serving size. If the label serving size is $1/2$ cup, and you eat one cup, you are getting twice the calories, fat, and other nutrients listed.

✦ Controlling the amount and type of fat you eat will help lower your risk for heart disease. Eating more plant foods can also help. Research shows that eating a wide variety of fruits, vegetables, beans, nuts, and whole grains is protective against disease. Along with vitamins, minerals, and nutrients, these foods are great sources of dietary fiber.

✦ Dietary fiber is a general term that describes the part of plant foods that your body cannot digest. Soluble fiber, found in foods such as oatmeal, oat bran, psyllium, beans, peas, barley, citrus fruits, and apples has been shown to reduce blood cholesterol levels. Insoluble fiber, like that in wheat, corn, and rice, does not have a cholesterol lowering effect but is protective against colon cancer. Dietary fiber prevents constipation and promotes a feeling of fullness. Reducing fat intake while increasing fiber can benefit anyone who wants to lose or maintain weight. The recommended daily allowance of dietary fiber for men is 30 to 38 grams per day and 21 to 25 grams for women.

Here are some steps you can take to boost your fiber intake:

Step 1: Eat more fruit. Eat more than 2 cups per day.

✦ Eat fresh fruit more often instead of canned, peeled, or juices.

✦ Top whole grain cereal with $\frac{1}{2}$ sliced banana for breakfast.

✦ Make a fruit smoothie with fresh or frozen berries, banana, juice, or yogurt.

✦ Add apples, mandarin oranges, raisins, or pears to tossed salads. (See Green Salad with Fresh Pears, Feta, and Raspberry Vinaigrette, page 92.)

Step 2: Eat more vegetables. Strive for 3 cups per day.

✦ Eat two or more meatless, vegetable-rich meals a week.

✦ Eat at least 2 vegetables (½ cup =1 serving) and a salad every night.

✦ Have baby carrots and sugar snap peas on hand for snacks.

✦ Keep frozen veggies on hand for quick stir-fries, or to add to soups, stews, or pasta dishes.

✦ Grill, roast, or broil vegetables in the oven with a touch of olive oil. Try new potatoes, sweet potatoes, eggplant, zucchini, red bell pepper, carrots, etc. (See page 211.)

✦ Order pizza with vegetable toppings.

Step 3: Eat more beans/legumes and whole grains.

✦ Make half your grains whole.

✦ Use whole wheat pasta and brown rice.

✦ Choose breads and cereals labeled "whole wheat" or "whole grain" as the first ingredient.

✦ Eat hot oat bran, oatmeal, and whole grain cereals instead of refined ones.

✦ Add kidney beans to salads.

✦ Make beans your main entrée.

(See Minestrone Soup, page 60.)

✦ A heart healthy lifestyle, one that includes regular physical activity and a gradual change in eating habits, is not easy, but it is well worth it. Choose to make the steps necessary to reduce your risk for disease. Begin incorporating recipes from this cookbook and you will be one step closer to a healthier heart.

15

Herbs and Spices

Herbs

Herbs are plants that are used for flavoring or garnishing in cooking, for medicinal purposes and for making perfumes and potpourris. Charlemagne described an herb as, "The friend of the physician and the pride of cooks."

Herbs are very helpful in salt-free diets. Even though my family is not required to be on a salt-free diet, I enjoy cooking with herbs, and I often experiment with different combinations. As a gardener, they are some of my favorite plants to grow.

Herbs may be used fresh or dried. When using fresh herbs, they are not as potent, so you need to use more. Cut fresh herbs very fine with kitchen shears to help blend their flavor with the food.

Here are some suggestions for using herbs in your cooking:

Anise (licorice-flavored seeds) – Use to flavor many dishes, casseroles, vegetables, cookies, or cakes. Store sugar in an airtight container overnight with anise seeds, then use the sugar in sugar cookies, pancakes, or hot toast. If you don't want anise seeds in your food, use anisette, an anise-flavored liqueur.

Basil – Use with fish, Italian dishes, chicken, fresh tomatoes, squash, peas, carrots, cauliflower, salads, and tomatoes. Or make your own basil vinegar.

Bay leaves – Use in beans, soups, chicken, rice, and cooked red cabbage. Always remove the leaf before serving because it is unpalatable.

Burnet – Use in salads and salad dressings.

Chervil – Use in chowder, chicken, tuna, salads, mashed potatoes, soups, zucchini, bread dough, vegetable dips, or sprinkle over fresh tomatoes.

Cilantro – Use in salads, Mexican foods, salsa,

and soups. Cilantro has a distinctive flavor, so use with caution.

Coriander – Use with apple pie or other apple dishes and sugar cookies.

Dill – Use in biscuits, rolls, or any homemade bread, salads, freshly sliced cucumbers, fresh tomatoes, vegetable dips, asparagus, green beans, cooked potatoes, potato salad, beets, or fish. Or make your own dill vinegar.

Garlic – Use in vegetable dips, chicken, Italian dishes, Mexican dishes, fish, and soup.

Ginger – Use with carrots or in gingerbread. Also use fresh for stir-fried dishes. Substitute fresh ginger in recipes that call for ground ginger; use about half the amount called for.

Marjoram – Use with zucchini, soup, chicken, and biscuits. Sprinkle over fresh tomatoes—basic in Italian dishes.

Mint – Use in peas, pea soup, fruit, or as a garnish for iced tea.

Oregano – Use in bread dough, Italian dishes, Mexican dishes, and with zucchini.

Parsley – Use in salads, bread dough, new potatoes, creamed potatoes, vegetable dips, soup, rice, fish, meatballs, and chicken.

Rosemary – Use in chicken, biscuits, stuffing, green beans, and rice.

Sage – Use in chicken, meat loaf, rice, stuffing, and gravy.

Tarragon – Use with fish, chicken, in sauces, vegetable dips, salad, or green beans. Or make your own tarragon vinegar.

Thyme – Use in chicken, stuffing, rice, beets, carrots, and green beans.

Herb vinegar

Herb vinegar is easy to make and fun to experiment with. As a general rule, put 1 cup fresh, clean herbs in a 1-quart glass jar. Add enough vinegar to cover the herbs. Cover and let steep for about two weeks. Check occasionally to be sure all the herbs are covered by vinegar. If not, add more vinegar.

The longer you let the vinegar and herbs steep, the stronger the flavor. When you are pleased with the flavor, strain the vinegar.

To avoid the chances of a chemical reaction, only use glass jars with nonmetal tops, such as decanters or wine bottles.

Bouquet garni

Bouquet garni is generally used in soups, stews, or foods that must be cooked for a long period. It is also used in recipes where you want the flavor without any bits of herbs. Tie herbs in a piece of cheesecloth and add to the food. When finished cooking, remove the bag and discard.

You can use any combination of herbs for a bouquet garni, or keep the traditional combination on hand. It calls for bay leaf, parsley, marjoram, and thyme. I also like to add one or two garlic cloves.

Spices

Spices are commonly used to flavor food. They have a strong, pungent flavor. Unlike herbs, which can be easily grown in home gardens, spices are usually imported. The aroma always conjures up foreign, exotic places in my mind.

Below are some suggestions for using spices in your cooking:

Allspice – Use with chicken crêpes, fruit crêpes, fresh fruit, rice pudding, fruit dips, marinara sauce, and French toast.

Black pepper – Whole peppercorns, freshly ground, are very pungent. Ground black pepper loses its punch faster. Use in meat and vegetable dishes.

Cayenne pepper – Made from the hottest chile peppers, which are small and vary in color from yellow to red. Use with chicken, beans, Mexican dishes, and barbecue sauce.

Lemon pepper – Blend of dried lemon rind and ground black pepper. Use with chicken, fish, dips, and seafood chowder.

Red pepper – Made from larger, less pungent (but still hot) peppers. Use in chicken, fish, dried beans, and Mexican and Italian dishes.

Chili powder – Blend of chile peppers, oregano, cumin, garlic powder, salt, and onion powder. Use with chicken, dried beans, and Mexican dishes.

Cinnamon – Use with blueberries, apple dishes, pumpkin, peaches, cherries, fruit salad, fruit dips, cakes, gingerbread, cookies, pies, rice pudding, and French toast.

Cloves – Use with pumpkin, apple, fruit salad, fruit dips, chicken salad, red cabbage, and French toast.

Curry powder – Blend of several pungent, exotic spices. Use with chicken, seafood, rice, cocktail sauces, and dips.

Nutmeg – Use with sweet potatoes, pumpkin, spinach, quiche, peas, carrots, sauces, fruit pies, and rice pudding.

Paprika – Sprinkle on fish, chicken, or vegetables. Add a dash of color as well as flavor.

Saffron – Very expensive, but it goes a long way. Use with chicken and rice.

Turmeric – Use with salads, coleslaw, and chicken. Also good to add a bit of yellow coloring to foods.

Special Menus

Brunch

Variety of chilled juices

Fresh Fruit Kabobs, *page 43*

Miniature Crab Quiche, *page 40*

Mixed green salad

Sweet-and-Sour Dressing, *page 119*

Blueberry Tea Cake, *page 269*

Tea or coffee

Special Occasion Breakfast

Grapefruit half

French Toast with Steamed Apples, *page 86*

Maple syrup

Skim milk

Tea or coffee

Weekday Breakfast

Chilled orange juice

Cornflakes sprinkled with Bran Buds

$1/2$ banana, sliced over cereal

Oat-Bran Muffin, *page 69*

Any Day Breakfast

Orange slices

Scrambled Egg Beaters

Whole wheat toast

Strawberry jelly

Breakfast for a Cold Winter Day

Steamed prunes

Oatmeal

Raisin bread toast

Skim milk

Saturday Breakfast

Grapefruit juice

Pancakes, *page 84*

Maple syrup

Skim milk

Ladies' Luncheon

Curried Chicken and Pasta Salad, *page 111*

Fresh melon wedges

Whole Wheat Molasses Bread, *page 76*

Lemon Snow Pudding, *page 303*

Variety of herbal teas, hot or cold

Lunch for a Summer Day

Tuna Salad sandwich, *page 97*
Honey Whole Wheat Bread, *page 78*
Pickled Beets and Onions, *page 109*
Pineapple-Cherry Sherbet, *page 307*
Iced mint tea

Lunch for a Cold Day

Baked Corn Chips
Chicken Chili, *page 148*
Spinach Apple Salad, *page 99*
Reduced-fat raspberry-walnut
salad dressing
Fresh orange wedges
Hot tea

Lunch for the Garden Club

Assorted fresh vegetables
Herb Dip, *page 29*
Tropical Tuna Salad, *page 98*
Oatmeal Muffins, *page 71*
Pineapple Bavarian, *page 304*
Spiced iced tea with lemon wedge

Vegetarian Lunch

Vegetable Tostadas, *page 196*
Assorted fresh fruit
Fresh Fruit Dip, *page 33*

Prepare-Ahead Lunch

Minestrone, *page 60*
Chipped Turkey Sandwich, *page 254*
Carrot sticks
Fresh fruit

Weekday Dinner

Coleslaw, *page 94*
Salmon Patties, *page 176*
Rice and Green Onion, *page 221*
Gingered Carrots, *page 210*
Corn Bread, *page 73*
Apples and Cranberries, *page 292*

Dinner for a Busy Day

(Prepare the entire meal the day before)
Assorted fresh vegetables
Pumpernickel-Spinach Dip, *page 36*
Frozen Cabbage Salad, *page 101*
Chicken and Vegetable Casserole, *page 137*
Dilly Bread, *page 77*

Dinner on the Grill

Pennsylvania Dutch Tomatoes and Onions,
page 113
Grilled Salmon, *page 182*
Corn on the cob
Sourdough rolls
Sparkling Fruit Cup, *page 104*

Italian Dinner

Garbanzo Bean Spread, *page 27*

Pasta with Chicken, *page 145*

Mixed green salad

Reduced-Fat Italian dressing

Hot Garlic Bread, *page 80*

Fresh fruit

Wine

Vegetarian Dinner

Stuffed Cherry Tomatoes, *page 42*

Vegetarian Lasagna, *page 193*

Mixed green salad

Vinegar and Oil Dressing, *page 120*

Rye bread

Baked Pears and Raisins, *page 297*

Dinner in a Hurry

Sliced tomatoes

So-Easy Fish, *page 165*

Oven French Fries, *page 219*

Vegetable combination (frozen foods)

French bread

Fresh fruit

Fresh Fruit Dip, *page 33*

Casual Company Dinner

Pumpernickel-Spinach Dip, *page 36*

Mixed green salad

Reduced-fat Italian dressing

Chicken-Stuffed Pasta Shells, *page 147*

Jean's Italian Bread, *page 179*

Blueberry and Peach Crisp, *page 293*

White wine

Special Company Dinner

Fresh vegetables

Horseradish Dip, *page 34*

Sparkling Fruit Cup, *page 104*

Coq au Vin, *page 131*

Brown Rice Pilaf, *page 205*

Green Beans and Dill, *page 201*

Dinner Rolls, *page 82*

White wine

Thanksgiving Dinner

Cranberry-Orange Salad, *page 103*

Roast turkey

Chicken Gravy, *page 235*

Mashed potatoes

Pennsylvania Sweet Potatoes in Tangy Sauce, *page 218*

Broccoli or green beans

Dinner Rolls, *page 82*

Apples and Cranberries, *page 292*

Reduced-fat whipped topping

Hawaiian Buffet

Audrey's Oriental Chicken, *page 152*

Brown Rice Pilaf, *page 205*

Gingered Carrots, *page 210*

Green Beans and Dill, *page 201*

Hot crispy rolls

Piña Colada Crêpes, *page 311*

Easter Buffet

Sparkling Fruit Cup, *page 104*

Grilled Asparagus, *page 224*

Baked turkey breast

New potatoes with parsley

Fresh green peas

Homemade Biscuits, *page 67*

Pineapple-Cherry Upside-Down
    Cake, *page 275*

Christmas Eve Supper

Green Salad with Fresh Pears, Feta,
    and Raspberry Vinaigrette, *page 92*

Hearty Chicken Noodle Soup, *page 57*

Hot crusty bread

Assorted holiday cookies

Summer Sunday Supper

Fresh Fruit Kabobs, *page 43*

Grilled Chicken with Herbs, *page 141*

Grandma's Potato Salad, *page 110*

Oatmeal Muffins, *page 71*

Lemonade

Winter Sunday Supper

Waldorf Salad, *page 115*

Clam Corn Chowder, *page 56*

Johnny's Oatmeal Cake, *page 270*

Hot spiced tea

Appetizers

I **have created appetizers** that are both nutritious and appealing. No longer will you have to be concerned about appetizers and snacks that are high in all the "no-nos."

Children who are not particularly fond of fresh fruit suddenly can't get enough when they have Fresh Fruit Dip to "dunk" the fruit in. They also love fresh vegetables with dip and Quesadillas with warm melted reduced-fat cheese. Keep a basket of fresh fruit on the table or within easy reach. Colorful and fresh fruit appeals to children and adults.

For nourishing, quick additions to a lunch box or an afterschool snack, fill attractive glass jars with carrot sticks, celery sticks, and zucchini wedges. Keep them in the refrigerator for snackers. To serve the same purpose, keep a supply of small rice cakes and crisp flat breads in the cabinet. Most children are just as happy to munch on these feather-light snacks as on cholesterol-heavy crackers. Read every label to make sure snacks conform to your diet.

Give your family a variety of nutritious foods to choose from and make all these foods easy to see and reach.

Following are appetizers that can be prepared and presented in a minimum of time:

✦ Try thinly sliced smoked turkey breast, served on crisp flat bread, garnished with a tiny sweet pickle.

✦ If your diet permits smoked oysters, try cherry tomatoes stuffed with smoked oysters that have been dipped in seafood sauce.

✦ Crab is so versatile but not always available to everyone; however, imitation or canned crab is a great substitute for fresh. You don't have to put forth much effort when serving crab—it is delicious in many different treatments. Serve crab on wooded picks with seafood cocktail sauce, or topped with reduced–fat cream cheese topped with seafood cocktail sauce.

Appetizers are to stimulate the appetite, not satisfy it. How many times have you spent days preparing for a dinner party only to watch your guests indulge in too many appetizers and not be hungry for the remainder of the meal? Watch the quantity, don't make too many and don't pass them around too many times.

Marinated Vegetables

Works well on your favorite vegetables or spoon over green salad.

3	cups prepared vegetables of choice
5	slices red onion
$1/2$	cup no-oil Italian dressing
1	teaspoon chopped pimiento
$1/4$	teaspoon celery seeds
$1/2$	teaspoon Italian seasoning

In a medium saucepan or saucepans, steam vegetables of choice until barely tender; remove to a medium-size bowl. Separate onion slices into rings; mix into vegetables. In a small bowl, combine dressing, pimiento, celery seeds, and Italian seasoning. Mix well and pour over vegetables. Cover and refrigerate several hours or overnight. Arrange vegetables attractively on a serving platter with wooden picks available.

Yield: 12 ($1/4$-cup) servings

Vegetable ideas:

◆ Broccoli

◆ Cauliflower

◆ Mushrooms

◆ Zucchini chunks

1 serving contains: *Cal 12kc, Prot 1gm, Fat trace, Chol 0, Carb 2gm, Fib 1gm Sodium 24mg*

Garbanzo Bean Spread

Attractive and tasty when spread on celery or other vegetables.

In a medium bowl, combine the beans, 1 tablespoon bean liquid, garlic, oil, and lime juice. In a blender or food processor fitted with the metal blade, process the mixture until smooth; it may be necessary to process in two batches if using a blender. Scoop into the bowl. Stir in the red pepper sauce, yogurt, pimiento, salt, and pepper. Serve as desired.

Yield: 20 (1-tablespoon) servings

1 serving contains: *Cal 24kc, Prot 1gm, Fat 1gm, Chol trace, Carb 4gm, Fib 1gm, Sodium 110mg*

1   (15-ounce) can garbanzo beans, drained, 1 tablespoon liquid reserved

1   garlic clove, minced

1   teaspoon extra-virgin olive oil

1   teaspoon lime juice

Dash of red pepper sauce

2   tablespoons plain reduced-fat yogurt

2   tablespoons chopped pimiento

Salt and pepper to taste

Refried Bean Dip

A tasty addition to your next barbecue. Serve warm with baked corn chips or raw vegetables.

2 cups Refried Beans, page 208

¼ cup chopped onion

2 tablespoons chopped green chilies

½ cup salsa

In a medium-size saucepan, combine all ingredients. Heat over medium heat until bubbling. Or use a microwave oven. Serve as desired.

Yield: 18 (2-tablespoon) servings

1 serving contains: *Cal 7kc, Prot trace, Fat trace, Chol trace, Carb 1gm, Fib trace, Sodium 27mg*

Herb Dip

Sour cream with dill makes it special.

In a small bowl, combine all the ingredients. Cover and refrigerate for several hours. Serve with fresh vegetables or use as a topping for baked fish.

Yield: 28 (1-tablespoon) servings

1 serving contains: *Cal 24kc, Prot 1gm, Fat 2gm, Chol 5mg, Carb 1mg, Fib trace, Sodium 49mg*

1	cup reduced-fat sour cream
$3/4$	cup reduced-fat mayonnaise
1	teaspoon grated onion
1	teaspoon parsley flakes
1	teaspoon snipped chives
$1/2$	teaspoon dill weed
$1/8$	teaspoon garlic powder

Zippy Meat Balls
This special treat uses ground turkey.

1 pound ground turkey

About 1 cup fresh breadcrumbs

1/3 cup minced onion

2 egg whites, slightly beaten

1 tablespoon minced fresh parsley

Pepper to taste

1/2 teaspoon Worcestershire sauce

1/2 teaspoon olive oil

Sauce:

1 (12-ounce) bottle chili sauce

1 (10-ounce) jar grape jelly

1/4 teaspoon ground ginger

In a large bowl, combine the turkey, breadcrumbs, onion, egg whites, parsley, pepper, and Worcestershire sauce. This mixture needs to be fairly firm, so add more breadcrumbs if needed. Shape into 1-inch balls. Heat a large nonstick skillet, add the oil, then meatballs. Cook until done, turning gently to brown on all sides. Drain. To make the sauce, combine the chili sauce, jelly, and ginger in a medium-size saucepan. Heat over medium-low heat until the jelly is melted, stirring constantly. Add the meat balls; stir gently to coat all sides. Simmer, uncovered, 30 minutes. Serve in an ovenproof dish set on a heating tray with wooden picks.

Yield: About 17 (2-meat ball) servings

1 serving contains: *Cal 115kc, Prot 5gm, Fat 1gm, Chol 11mg, Carb 22mg, Fib trace, Sodium 333mg*

Shrimp Tortilla Rolls

For an attractive presentation, leave three shrimp whole, line tray with lettuce, place tortilla rolls on lettuce and arrange the shrimp in a cluster in the center.

Beat the cream cheese with a fork until creamy. Add the cilantro, horseradish, and lemon juice; blend well. Add the finely chopped shrimp; stir to blend.

Divide the mixture between tortillas spreading to cover each tortilla. Roll each tortilla jelly-roll style, wrap in plastic wrap, and refrigerate until ready to serve. When ready to serve, slice each roll into 8 slices, arrange on tray with cocktail sauce.

Yield 28 (2-roll) servings

1 serving contains: *Cal 102kc, Prot 5gm, Fat 4gm, Chol 22mg, Carb 12gm, Fib 1, Sodium 301mg*

1   (8-ounce) container reduced-fat cream cheese, softened

1   teaspoon cilantro or parsley

$1/4$ teaspoon creamed horseradish

$1/4$ teaspoon lemon juice

$1/4$ pound shrimp, peeled, cooked, and chopped fine

6   (8-inch) flour tortillas

1   cup seafood cocktail sauce or salsa

Chicken Salad Stuffed Eggs

An unusual twist for stuffed eggs.

4	boneless, skinless chicken breast halves, cooked
24	large hard-boiled eggs, peeled
1	cup reduced-fat mayonnaise
½	teaspoon salt
¼	teaspoon ground pepper
2	green onions, finely chopped
1	tablespoon chopped fresh parsley
1	tablespoon chopped fresh dill
2	tablespoons fresh lemon juice
Dash of paprika	

ulse the cooled chicken in batches in food processor 3 to 4 times to shred, set aside.

Slice the hard-boiled eggs in half lengthwise; remove the yolk and reserve for other use.

Combine the mayonnaise, salt, pepper, onions, parsley, dill, lemon juice, and paprika; stir to mix well. Pour over the chicken; toss gently and spoon chicken mixture into egg white halves; sprinkle with paprika. Cover and chill for 1 hour or more.

Yield 48 (½ egg) servings

1 serving contains: *57kc, Prot 8gm, Fat 2gm, Chol 18mg, Carb 1 gm, Fib 0, Sodium 104mg*

Fresh Fruit Dip

Delicious accompaniment for fresh fruit.

In a small bowl, combine all ingredients; refrigerate. Serve as a dip with fresh fruit.

Yield: 16 (1-tablespoon) servings

1 serving contains: *Cal 13kc, Prot 1gm, Fat trace, Chol 1mg, Carb 2mg, Fib 0, Sodium 10mg*

1	cup plain reduced-fat yogurt
1	tablespoon honey
$\frac{1}{8}$	teaspoon ground nutmeg
$\frac{1}{8}$	teaspoon ground allspice

Variation:

✦ **Indian Fruit Dip:** Substitute $\frac{1}{8}$ teaspoon ground ginger and $\frac{1}{8}$ teaspoon ground cloves for spices.

✦ **Almond Fruit Dip:** Omit honey and spices. Combine 1 package artificial sweetener and $\frac{1}{2}$ teaspoon almond flavoring with yogurt.

✦ **Coconut Fruit Dip:** Omit honey and spices. Combine 1 package artificial sweetener and $\frac{1}{2}$ teaspoon coconut flavoring with yogurt.

Horseradish Dip

Horseradish and mustard combination creates a perky taste.

1   cup reduced-fat
    sour cream
3/4 cup reduced-fat
    mayonnaise
1/2 teaspoon Worcestershire
    sauce
1 1/2 teaspoons grated onion
1   teaspoon dry mustard
1   teaspoon snipped chives
    or to taste
3/4 teaspoon prepared
    horseradish
1/2 teaspoon lemon pepper
1/2 teaspoon garlic powder
1   teaspoon parsley flakes

In a small bowl, combine all the ingredients. Cover and refrigerate for several hours. Serve as desired.

Yield: 28 (1-tablespoon) servings

1 serving contains: *Cal 24kc, Prot 1gm, Fat 2gm, Chol 5mg, Carb 1mg, Fib trace, Sodium 49mg*

Favorite Crabmeat Spread

This is great for an easy and quick appetizer.

Mix the cream cheese, mayonnaise, scallions, chili sauce, Worcestershire sauce, and crabmeat together. Spread on sliced, toasted baguette, or crackers; top with a tiny sprig of dill or parsley.

Yield: 12 (2-tablespoon) servings

1 serving contains: *Cal 69kc, Prot 5gm, Fat 4gm, Chol 23mg, Carb 2mg, Fib trace, Sodium 144mg*

8   ounces reduced-fat cream cheese, softened

2   tablespoons reduced-fat mayonnaise

3   scallions, finely chopped

2   tablespoons chili sauce

Dash of Worcestershire sauce

1   (6-ounce) can of white crabmeat

Sprigs of fresh dill or parsley, optional

Pumpernickel-Spinach Dip

Fun party food.

1	pound round loaf pumpernickel bread
1	cup reduced-fat sour cream
3/4	cup reduced-fat mayonnaise
1	(8-ounce) can water chestnuts, drained, finely chopped
1/2	cup minced onion
1	package Knorr's vegetable soup mix
1	teaspoon parsley flakes
1	(10-ounce) package thawed frozen chopped spinach, well drained

Cut the top off the loaf and carefully remove most of the bread inside, leaving a shell. In a large bowl, combine the remaining ingredients. Cover and refrigerate for several hours. To serve, spoon the filling into the hollowed-out loaf of bread. Serve with the remaining bread, cut into cubes.

Yield: 16 ($^1/_4$-cup) servings

1 serving contains: *Cal 129kc, Prot 5gm, Fat 4gm, Chol 6mg, Carb 20gm, Fib 2gm, Sodium 321mg*

Fresh Onion Dip

Excellent when served warm.

Heat the oil in a large nonstick skillet over medium heat. When hot add the onions and salt. Cook, uncovered, for 20 minutes until slightly browned, stirring occasionally. Stir in the sage and remove from the heat; stir in the sour cream and Parmesan cheese. Transfer to a serving bowl and sprinkle with chives. Serve immediately with crackers, baked tortilla chips, or toasted baguette.

Yield: 8 (2 tablespoons) servings

1 serving contains: *Cal 100kc, Prot 2gm, Fat 7gr, Chol 5mg, Carb 9gm, Fib 1g, Sodium 193 mg*

2 tablespoons extra-virgin olive oil

2 cups chopped onions

$1/2$ teaspoon salt

2 teaspoon snipped fresh sage or 1 teaspoon dried sage

$1/3$ cup reduced-fat sour cream

2 tablespoon grated Parmesan cheese

2 tablespoon finely chopped chives

Southwest Spicy Roll-ups

Sure to be a big hit with your family or guests.

1 (8-ounce) container reduced-fat cream cheese
3 tablespoons reduced-fat sour cream
1 teaspoon lime juice
5 green onions, finely chopped
1/4 cup chopped, pitted, ripe olives, drained
1 cup salsa, divided*
10 (8-inch) flour tortillas

Bring the cream cheese to room temperature. Add the sour cream, lime juice, onions, olives, and just enough salsa to make spreadable. Stir to blend well. Spread the mixture over the tortillas; roll up jelly-roll style, place on plastic wrap, wrapping tightly; refrigerate until just before serving. Slice and serve with the remaining salsa.

* You can use mild, medium, or hot salsa according to your taste.

Yield: 40 (1-inch slice) servings

1 serving contains: *Cal 64kc, Prot 1gm, Fat 2gr, Cho 14mg, Carb 3gm, Fib 0, Sodium 88mg*

Grace's Chicken Wings

So good you won't be able to stop with just one!

Preheat the oven to 400°F (205°C). Using kitchen shears, cut the drumette from the remainder of the wing on each piece of chicken. (The drumette is the largest section of the chicken wing.) Save the scrappy pieces for broth. Place the chicken drumettes on a broiler pan with a rack. Bake for 25 minutes. In a saucepan, combine the sugar and cornstarch; add the ginger, lemon peel, pepper, onion powder, water, lemon juice, and soy sauce. Cook over medium heat until the mixture starts to simmer; cook for 3 to 4 minutes longer. Pour the sauce over the chicken. Cover and refrigerate until almost serving time. Bake in a preheated 400°F (205°C) oven for 30 minutes until browned and heated. Serve garnished with lemon slices in an ovenproof dish set on a heating tray.

24 chicken wings, about 3 pounds
1 cup sugar
3 tablespoons cornstarch
$1/2$ teaspoon ground ginger
$1/4$ teaspoon grated lemon peel
$1/4$ teaspoon pepper
$1/8$ teaspoon onion powder
$3/4$ cup water
$1/3$ cup lemon juice
$1/4$ cup low-sodium soy sauce
Lemon slices for garnish

Yield: 24 servings

1 serving contains: *Cal 135kc, Prot 9gm, Fat 7gm, Chol 29mg, Carb 9gm, Fib trace, Sodium 200mg*

Miniature Crab Quiche

Avoid the high cholesterol of traditional quiche.

Pastry dough for 1 Piecrust*
made with corn oil, page 302

1 egg white

1/4 cup egg substitute

1/4 cup evaporated
skim milk

1/4 cup shredded
reduced-fat
Swiss cheese

1 tablespoon minced green
onion, green
and white parts

1/8 teaspoon salt

1/8 teaspoon ground
marjoram

1/8 teaspoon ground
lemon pepper

1/2 cup finely chopped crab
or imitation crab

1/4 cup grated
Parmesan cheese

Preheat the oven to 400°F (205°C). Lightly grease two pans of miniature muffin cups (24 muffin cups). Roll the pastry dough between two sheets of wax paper until quite thin. Using a 2½-inch round cutter, cut the dough into circles and fit into the miniature muffin cups. Prick the crusts. Bake for 2 minutes, prick again and bake for 2 minutes longer. Remove the crusts from the oven; reduce the oven temperature to 350°F (175°C). Combine the egg white, egg substitute, evaporated milk, cheese, green onion, salt, marjoram, lemon pepper, and imitation crab in a medium bowl. Spoon the mixture into the miniature quiche crusts; sprinkle with the Parmesan cheese. Bake for about 20 minutes or until set. Let set in the pan for 5 minutes before carefully removing to a serving tray.

Yield: 24 servings (1 quiche each)

* You can substitute piecrust from the dairy case.

1 serving contains: Cal 60kc, Prot 3gm, Fat 3gm, Chol 2mg, Carb 5gm, Fib trace, Sodium 69mg

Nachos

Great addition to a Mexican-style dinner.

Preheat the oven to 400°F (205°C). Cut each tortilla into 8 wedges; place on a large baking sheet. Bake for about 5 minutes, turn and bake for 5 minutes longer or until crisp. Sprinkle the cheese evenly over the chips, then lightly sprinkle the salsa over the cheese. Bake for 4 to 5 minutes longer, or until the cheese is melted.

Yield: 4 (1-cup) servings

8	(6-inch) corn tortillas (made with corn oil or without lard)
3/4	cup shredded reduced-fat Cheddar cheese
3	tablespoons salsa

Variation:

✦ For extra spice, add a few thin slices of jalapeño pepper on top of salsa.

1 serving contains: *Cal 198kc, Prot 11gm, Fat 6gm, Chol 15mg, Carb 28gm, Fib 2gm, Sodium 306mg,*

Stuffed Cherry Tomatoes

Rich in vitamins, low in fat.

25 cherry tomatoes,
about 1 pound, washed,
dried

3/4 cup reduced-fat
sour cream

1/4 teaspoon garlic powder

2 tablespoons minced
chives

1/4 teaspoon dill weed

Leaf lettuce

Dash of paprika, or to taste

Cut an X across top of each tomato and down sides, being careful not to cut through to the bottom. Scoop out half of the pulp from each tomato, save for use in another dish. Set the tomatoes cut side down on paper towels to drain. In a small bowl, combine the sour cream, garlic powder, chives, and dill weed. With a small spoon, carefully stuff the tomatoes with the herb mixture. Arrange on a platter lined with leaf lettuce and sprinkle with paprika. Refrigerate for 4 to 6 hours until ready to serve.

Yield: 25 servings

1 serving contains: *Cal 11kc, Prot 1gm, Fat 1gm, Chol 3mg, Carb 1gm, Fib trace, Sodium 28mg*

Fresh Fruit Kabobs

Terrific served with Fresh Fruit Dip, page 33.

Divide the fruit among 10 wooden skewers, alternating different fruits. Refrigerate for 2 hours until serving time. To serve, arrange the skewers on a platter lined with leaf lettuce. Garnish with mint sprigs.

Yield: 10 servings

1 serving contains: *Cal 45kc, Prot 1gm, Fat trace, Chol 0, Carb 11gm, Fib 2gm, Sodium 1mg*

1	fresh pineapple, cubed, about 2 cups
2	cups fresh strawberries, washed and drained, not hulled
3	oranges, peeled and sectioned

Leaf lettuce

Mint sprigs for garnish

Quesadillas

Quick and easy appetizer or great with a green salad for a weekend supper.

4	large flour tortillas
1	cup (4 ounces) shredded reduced-fat Cheddar cheese
2	ounces green chilies

Heat a large nonstick skillet over medium heat; add a tortilla and heat briefly. Sprinkle with $1/2$ cup of the cheese and about half the chilies, top with another tortilla. Heat until the cheese is melted, pressing together lightly. Repeat with the remaining tortillas. To serve, cut in half or in quarters.

Yield: 4 servings ($^1/_2$ quesadilla each)

1 serving contains: *Cal 178kc, Prot 11gm, Fat 6gm, Chol 20mg, Carb 19 mg, Fib 0, Sodium 210mg*

Soups

omemade soups are a wonderful source of good nutrition— when a wise choice of ingredients, vitamins, fiber, and minerals fill the soup pot. Soups in this section have been chosen because they are low in fat and cholesterol and high in taste appeal.

You can make a broth almost fat-free by chilling it and removing the layer of solid fat that conveniently rises to the surface. You can add nutrition by saving the water from cooking vegetables and freezing it to boost a soup at a later date. You can also add leftover vegetables to soups. Substitute herbs and spices for that extra dash of salt, and you will increase the flavor and decrease the sodium. To add a little body to a soup, use whole grains and egg-yolk-free pastas.

Use your imagination—be creative. Make a pot of soup from scratch and enjoy it for lunch or as the main dish for dinner with a salad and some home-baked or bakery bread. Make a large pot and freeze the extra to use later. You can always stretch soup with leftovers that might not be enough for a complete meal.

Hint for Preparing Dried Beans

✦ Beans can bring variety and extra nutrition to your menu for such a small price. They are high in protein, magnesium, vitamins, and fiber, and are low in fat and easy to store.

✦ Most dried beans should be soaked overnight to restore the water lost in drying, and this will also shorten the cooking time. When soaking beans, use a large container to allow for expansion of the beans. Use at least 6 cups of water for each pound of dried beans.

✦ If you forget to presoak the beans, place them in boiling water and boil for 3 minutes, then let them stand, covered, for 1 to 2 hours. Rinse and proceed with your recipe.

✦ If you have a problem with beans "talking back" to you, try the following hint: Discard the soaking water, cover the beans with fresh water and cook for 30 minutes. Discard that water, add more fresh water and a pinch of ginger, then proceed to cook until beans are tender.

✦ One pound of dried beans equals 2 cups in volume. Dried beans double in weight and volume when cooked so 2 cups dried beans will give you 4 cups cooked beans.

✦ For tender beans, cover over a low heat and do not add salt until the beans are almost cooked. If the beans appear to be drying out, add more water during cooking.

✦ You can add chopped onion, garlic, stewed tomatoes, or a little olive oil to add extra flavor to the beans.

Chilled Rhubarb Soup

Serve this colorful soup before or after dinner.

Place the rhubarb in a medium-size saucepan. In a small bowl, blend the cornstarch and water; add to rhubarb. Cover and bring to a boil over medium heat; reduce the heat to low and cook for 10 minutes or until tender. Add the sugar, cinnamon, allspice, and wine. Pour into a blender or food processor fitted with the metal blade; process for about 20 seconds or until smooth. Refrigerate for 2 to 8 hours until ready to serve. To serve, pour the soup into 4 individual bowls. Top the soup in each bowl with 1 teaspoon yogurt; gently swirl the yogurt to make an attractive design.

Yield: 4 ($^1/_2$-cup) servings

2	cups cubed rhubarb, fresh or frozen
1	tablespoon cornstarch
2	cups water
$^1/_4$	cup plus 1 tablespoon sugar
$^1/_8$	teaspoon ground cinnamon
$^1/_8$	teaspoon ground allspice
2	tablespoons Marsala wine
4	teaspoons plain reduced-fat yogurt

Variation:

✦ **Chilled Blueberry Soup:** Substitute 2 cups fresh or frozen blueberries for rhubarb; reduce sugar to 3 tablespoons.

1 serving contains: *Cal 90kc, Prot 1gm, Fat trace, Chol trace, Carb 21gm, Fib 0, Sodium 7mg*

Chilled Cherry Soup

Great on a hot summer day.

1	(1-pound) can red sour cherries, pitted
2	teaspoons cornstarch
1/4	cup sugar
1/8	teaspoon ground cinnamon
1 1/2	teaspoons finely grated orange peel
1/2	cup orange juice
2	tablespoons Marsala wine
4	teaspoons reduced-fat sour cream

Pour the cherries and juice into a blender or food processor fitted with the metal blade; process for about 20 seconds or until smooth to make cherry purée. Pour into a medium-size saucepan; set aside. In a small bowl, combine the cornstarch, sugar, and cinnamon. Stir in a little cherry purée. When blended, stir into the saucepan with the remaining cherry purée. Add 1 teaspoon orange peel and orange juice. Bring to a boil over medium heat; reduce heat to low and cook about 2 minutes, stirring constantly. Stir in the wine. Refrigerate 2 to 8 hours until ready to serve. To serve, pour the soup into 4 individual bowls. Top the soup in each bowl with 1 teaspoon sour cream and sprinkle with remaining orange peel.

Yield: 4 (1/2-cup) servings

1 serving contains: *Cal 132kc, Prot 4gm, Fat trace, Chol 1mg, Carb 29gm, Fib trace, Sodium 87mg*

Black-Eyed Pea Soup

Plays an important role in our New Year's dinner because—according to Southern tradition—black-eyed peas bring good luck.

The night before, sort and wash the peas; put in a large kettle. Add the water to cover and soak overnight in a cool place. The next morning, discard the soaking water and add 6 cups fresh water to cover. Add the remaining ingredients and cook over low heat for 2 hours or until beans are tender. Serve immediately.

Yield: 16 (1/2-cup) servings

Optional:

✦ **To add even more nutrition, about 25 minutes before peas are ready add sauted green or red bell pepper, 1 cup of brown rice and 2 to 3 cups of water. Cover and cook on low heat until rice is tender.**

1 serving contains: *Cal 29kc, Prot 2gm, Fat 1gm, Chol 0, Carb 4gm, Fib trace, Sodium 240mg*

1	pound black-eyed peas
6	cups water
1/2	cup minced onion
1	bay leaf
1	teaspoon salt
Dash of red pepper sauce or to taste	
1	tablespoon extra-virgin olive oil
2	beef bouillon cubes
1	garlic clove, crushed

Chicken Corn Chowder

Begs for a tossed green salad to accompany it.

3	boneless, skinless chicken breasts halves
1	bay leaf
3/4	teaspoon dried thyme
1/2	teaspoon salt
1/8	teaspoon dried marjoram
2	garlic cloves, minced
1	tablespoon parsley flakes
1/4	teaspoon pepper
3	quarts water
2	chicken bouillon cubes
1	cup chopped celery
1	cup chopped onion
1	cup chopped carrot
2	cups whole kernel corn, fresh or frozen
2	cups Baking Mix,* page 66
2/3	cup water*

In a soup kettle, combine the chicken, bay leaf, thyme, salt, marjoram, garlic, parsley, pepper, and water. Cover and bring to a boil over high heat. Reduce the heat to medium low and cook for about 45 minutes. Add the bouillon cubes, celery, and onion; cook for about 15 minutes longer or until the chicken is tender. Remove the chicken from the broth; cool. Chop the chicken into medium-size chunks; set aside. Add the carrots to the broth and cook until almost tender, adding corn during the final few minutes. Adjust the heat to get a gentle boil. In a medium-size bowl, combine the Baking Mix and 2/3 cup water; stir with a fork until it forms a soft dough. Drop by the teaspoon into boiling kettle of vegetables. Cook, uncovered, over a low heat for 10 minutes, then cover and cook for about 10 minutes longer. Add the chicken and heat through. Serve immediately.

Yield: 14 (1-cup) servings

❋ You can substitute Reduced-Fat Bisquick and 2/3 cup skim milk instead of water.

1 serving contains: *116kc, Prot 8gm, Fat 2gm, Chol 16mg, Carb 16mg, Fib 1gm, Sodium 467mg*

New England-Style Clam Chowder

A family favorite, now with less fat.

In a large soup kettle over medium heat, cook the onion and celery in 1 tablespoon chicken broth until tender. Add the remaining chicken broth and potatoes; cook until tender. Add the clam nectar, lemon pepper, black pepper, garlic powder, and parsley; bring to a gentle boil. In a quart jar with a lid, combine the skim milk, flour, and cornstarch; shake until smooth. Slowly add to the soup, stirring constantly, until it starts to thicken. Add the clams and heat through; do not boil. Serve immediately.

Yield: 8 (1-cup) servings

* You can substitute 1/2 cup fat-free half-and-half for 1/2 cup skim milk.

1 serving contains: *Cal 168kc, Prot 13 gm, Fat 2gm, Chol 59mg, Carb 24gm, Fib 1gm, Sodium 296mg,*

1/2	cup chopped onion
1/2	cup chopped celery
2	cups reduced-fat, reduced-sodium chicken broth
2	cups diced potatoes
2	cups clam nectar
1/4	teaspoon lemon pepper
1/8	teaspoon freshly ground black pepper
1/8	teaspoon garlic powder
1/2	tablespoon parsley flakes
2 1/2	cups skim milk*
5	tablespoons all-purpose flour
3	tablespoons cornstarch
2	cups minced clams, fresh or canned

Chicken Gumbo

Makes a light, nutritious lunch.

$1/2$ cup chopped onion

$1/2$ cup chopped celery

4 cups reduced-fat, reduced-sodium chicken broth

2 cups stewed tomatoes

$1/4$ cup uncooked long-grain white rice

$1/2$ cup chopped green bell pepper

1 cup sliced okra

1 bay leaf

$1/4$ teaspoon salt

Pepper to taste

1 cup chopped cooked chicken breast

In a large soup kettle over medium heat, cook the onion and celery in 1 tablespoon chicken broth. Add the remaining chicken broth, tomatoes, and rice; bring to a boil. Reduce the heat to low and cook for 10 minutes. Add the green pepper, okra, bay leaf, salt, and pepper; cook for about 45 minutes or until the vegetables are tender. Add the chicken and heat through. Serve immediately.

Yield: 10 (1-cup) servings

1 serving contains: *Cal 85kc, Prot 9gm, Fat 1gm, Chol 15mg, Carb 10gm, Fib 1gm, Sodium 508mg*

Tortellini Soup

Place the green beans in a microwave-safe bowl, cover and microwave on high for 2 to 3 minutes, until tender. Place the beans, tomatoes, broth, garlic, and Italian seasoning in a large saucepan; bring to a boil; reduce the heat and simmer for five minutes. Add the tortellini, cook according to package instructions; stir in the parsley. When ready to serve; ladle the soup into bowls and sprinkle with mozzarella cheese and basil. Serve with crusty bread.

Yield: 6 servings

✳ You can use canned green beans or tomatoes

1 serving contains: *Cal 129, Prot 8, Fat 5gm, Chol 56mg, Carb 14gm, Fib 2gm, Sodium 703mg*

1	cup fresh green beans, broken into 1-inch pieces*
2	cups stewed tomatoes
2	(14-ounce) cans reduced-fat, reduced-sodium chicken broth
2	cloves garlic, minced
$1/2$	teaspoon Italian seasoning
1	(9-ounce) package refrigerated chicken tortellini, uncooked
1	tablespoon chopped fresh parsley
$1/4$	cup shredded reduced-fat, part skim mozzarella cheese
$1/4$	cup fresh basil, cut into strips

Clam Corn Chowder

A unique blending of flavors.

1	cup chopped onion
1	cup chopped celery
1/2	cup water
2	tomatoes, peeled, chopped, about 1 1/2 cups
2	tablespoons minced fresh parsley
2	cups cubed potatoes
1	teaspoon margarine or extra-virgin olive oil
4	ounces fresh mushrooms, thinly sliced
2	(10 1/2-ounce) cans reduced-fat, reduced-sodium cream of mushroom soup or 2 recipes Basic White Sauce with mushrooms, page 242
4	cups skim milk*
2	cups whole kernel corn
1/2	teaspoon lemon pepper
1/4	teaspoon black pepper
2	(6 1/2-ounce) cans minced clams, or 4 quarts unshucked fresh clams

In a large soup kettle over medium heat, cook the onion and celery in water until tender. Add the tomatoes, parsley, and potatoes; cook until tender. In a small nonstick skillet, heat the margarine; add the mushrooms and cook for 5 minutes. While the mushrooms are cooking, stir the soup or sauce, milk, corn, and peppers into the vegetables in the kettle. Reduce the heat to medium low and simmer for 10 minutes. Add the clams and mushrooms; simmer for 5 minutes longer. Serve immediately.

Yield: 12 (1-cup) servings

* Substitute 1 cup fat-free half-and-half for 1 cup of skim milk.

1 serving contains: *Cal 164kc, Prot 8gm, Fat 5gm, Chol 21mg, Carb 24gm, Fib 2gm, Sodium 496mg*

Hearty Chicken Noodle Soup

So hearty, you'll be tempted to eat it with a fork.

In a large soup kettle, place the chicken, water, bouillon cubes, garlic, bay leaf, thyme, parsley, salt, and pepper. Cover and bring to a boil over high heat. Reduce the heat to low and simmer for 45 to 50 minutes or until the chicken is tender. Remove the chicken to a plate; cool. Remove and discard the bone from the chicken. Cut the chicken into chunks; set aside. Add the carrot, celery, and onion to broth; simmer for about 30 minutes or until almost tender. Add the noodles and cook according to the package directions. Add the chicken during final few minutes to heat through. Serve immediately.

Yield: 12 (1-cup) servings

* Or you can use 3 boneless, skinless chicken breast halves.

1 serving contains: *Cal 111kc, Prot 9gm, Fat 1gm, Chol 30mg, Carb 15gm, Fib 2gm, Sodium 416mg*

1 1/2	whole chickens,* skinned
3	quarts water
2	chicken bouillon cubes
1	garlic clove, minced
1	bay leaf
3/4	teaspoon dried thyme
1	tablespoon minced fresh parsley
1	teaspoon salt
1/4	teaspoon pepper
3	cups sliced carrot
2	cups sliced celery
1	cup chopped onion
8	ounces noodles, yolk-free if available

Joyce's Cream of Broccoli Soup

A delicate cream soup that's low in fat.

1	large bunch of broccoli, about 6 cups chopped
3 1/2	cups reduced-fat, reduced-sodium chicken broth
1/4	cup chopped onion
1/4	cup chopped celery
1/4	cup all-purpose flour
2	cups skim milk*
1/2	teaspoon salt
Pepper to taste	
Ground nutmeg to taste	

Rinse and chop broccoli, cutting through stems for faster cooking. In a soup kettle over medium heat, simmer the broccoli in the chicken broth until tender. Using a slotted spoon, lift the broccoli out of broth. Reserve several broccoli flowerets for garnish. Put the remaining broccoli, onion, and celery in a blender or a food processor fitted with a metal blade; process until smooth then set aside. In a jar with a lid, combine the flour and milk; shake until dissolved. Slowly add to the chicken broth, stirring until it starts to thicken slightly. Add the puréed broccoli mixture, salt, pepper, and nutmeg, stirring just until the soup starts to simmer; do not boil. Garnish with reserved broccoli flowerets before serving.

Yield: 6 (1-cup) servings

* Substitute 1 cup fat-free half-and-half for 1 cup skim milk.

1 serving contains: *Cal 96kc, Prot 9gm, Fat 1gm, Chol 2mg, Carb 14gm, Fib 3gm, Sodium 686mg*

Lentil Soup

A tasty, economical dish.

Sort and wash lentils. Place in a large container; add the cold water to cover and let soak for about 3 hours. Pour into a colander to drain. In a large soup kettle over medium-low heat, cook the onion and celery in $1/2$ cup water until tender. Add the lentils and enough water to cover them well; bring to a boil. Add the bay leaf and bouillon cubes; reduce the heat and simmer for about 1 hour. Add the salt, pepper, tomato sauce, vinegar, and Italian seasoning; simmer for about 30 minutes or until tender. Serve immediately.

Yield: 8 (1-cup) servings

1 serving contains: *Cal 87kc, Prot 6gm, Fat trace, Chol 0, Carb 16gm, Fib 4gm, Sodium 695mg*

1 $1/3$	cups dried lentils
1	cup chopped onion
1	cup chopped celery
$1/2$	cup water
1	bay leaf
3	beef bouillon cubes
1	teaspoon salt
$1/4$	teaspoon pepper
$1/2$	cup tomato sauce
1	tablespoon red wine vinegar
$1/2$	teaspoon Italian seasoning

Minestrone

A complete, nutritious meal in one pot.

$1^1/_2$	cups dried beans, navy or pintos
3	quarts water, divided
3	beef bouillon cubes*
$4^1/_2$	cups stewed tomatoes
$^1/_2$	cup tomato sauce
$^1/_3$	cup uncooked brown rice or elbow macaroni
$1^1/_2$	cups chopped celery
2	cups sliced carrot
1	cup chopped onion
2	garlic cloves, minced
2	tablespoons chopped fresh parsley
$^1/_2$	teaspoon dried thyme
$^1/_2$	teaspoon dried oregano
2	cups chopped cabbage
1	cup cubed zucchini

Sort and wash the beans. Place in a large kettle; add enough cold water to cover and soak overnight. The next day, rinse the beans and return to the large kettle; add $1^1/_2$ quarts water. Bring to a boil over high heat; reduce the heat and simmer until tender. Add the bouillon cubes. In a separate large kettle put the remaining $1^1/_2$ quarts water, tomatoes, and tomato sauce; bring to a boil. Add the rice and reduce heat; simmer for about 15 minutes. Add the celery, carrot, onion, garlic, parsley, thyme, and oregano; simmer for about 20 minutes. Add the cabbage and zucchini; cook for about 15 minutes or until all the vegetables are tender. Add the cooked beans and liquid; heat through. Serve immediately.

Yield: 12 (1-cup) servings

* Substitute 2 Knorr chicken bouillon cubes if desired.

1 serving contains: *Cal 118kc, Prot 6gm, Fat 1gm, Chol 0, Carb 24gm, Fib 5gm, Sodium 558mg*

Onion Soup

Combine with a sandwich for a great meal.

Put the broth in a large soup kettle; add the onions. Bring to a boil; reduce the heat and simmer for about 1½ hours. Add the garlic, nutmeg, and Worcestershire sauce; simmer for 10 minutes. In a small jar with a lid, combine the flour and water; shake until completely dissolved. Stirring constantly, slowly add the flour mixture to the soup; simmer for 5 minutes longer. To serve, preheat the broiler. Place ½ slice of bread in the bottom of 8 individual ovenproof soup bowls. Carefully ladle soup into the bowls. Sprinkle each serving with 1 tablespoon cheese. Place under the broiler until cheese is melted and starting to brown. Serve immediately.

Yield: 8 (1-cup) servings

1 serving contains: *Cal 161kc, Prot 10gm, Fat 4gm, Chol 5mg, Carb 22gm, Fib 3gm, Sodium 921mg*

2	quarts reduced-fat, reduced-sodium chicken broth
7	cups sliced sweet onions, about 4 medium-size onions
2	garlic cloves, minced
¼	teaspoon ground nutmeg
2	teaspoons Worcestershire sauce
2	teaspoons all-purpose flour
¼	cup water
4	slices French bread, cut in half
½	cup shredded part-skim-milk mozzarella cheese

Kale, White Bean, and Sweet Potato Soup

1 tablespoon extra-virgin olive oil

1 small onion, chopped

2 small leeks, rinsed and thinly sliced (white and light green parts)

2 small sprigs fresh rosemary

2 cloves garlic, minced

6 cups reduced-fat, reduced-sodium chicken broth

1 sweet potato, peeled and cut into $1/2$-inch cubes

$1/2$ cup elbow macaroni, or your choice of pasta

1 (15-ounce) can cannellini beans

$1/2$ bunch fresh greens, kale, chard, turnip greens*

$1/4$ teaspoon salt

$1/2$ teaspoon freshly ground pepper

Heat the olive oil in a soup kettle on medium heat. Add the onion, leeks, and rosemary; sauté until tender. Add the garlic, stirring, for about 30 seconds; add the broth and sweet potato. Cover and simmer until potato is just beginning to soften. Add the pasta, beans, greens, salt, and pepper; cook until greens are wilted and the potato and pasta are tender.

Yield: 6 (1-cup) servings

* If using turnip greens, you can add 2 small turnips to soup with sweet potato for a different flavor.

1 serving contains: *Cal 207kc, Prot 10gm, Fat 4gm, Chol 0mg, Carb 36gm, Fib 6gm, Sod 736mg*

Breads

With the emphasis on good nutrition and fiber in today's diet, whole grains are recognized as a popular ingredient in our diets. I have included Banana Bread, Out-Bran Muffins, and Honey Whole Wheat Bread because of their extra nutritional value and enjoyable taste. But I also enjoy other breads made with unbleached flour, such as Biscuits, Jean's Italian Bread, or Corn Bread. In these recipes you might want to try using part whole wheat, which will make a slightly heavier bread. These foods contain similar levels of protein, complex carbohydrates, vitamins, and minerals and are certainly not "junk food." So as long as bread conforms to your diet—enjoy!

Hints for Making Bread: When making bread, strong beating of the dough is a must. This can be accomplished either with the dough hook of a heavy-duty electric mixer or by hand using a large spoon. Kneading also can be done either by a heavy-duty mixer or by hand on a lightly floured counter top. Test the dough by making an indentation with your finger; if the dough springs back, it has been kneaded enough. Put the dough in a warm, lightly greased bowl, cover with a cloth and set in a draft-free place to rise. When the dough has doubled in size, press your finger lightly into the dough. If an indentation remains, the dough is ready to shape. Turn out the dough onto a lightly floured surface. Knead it for a minute or two, shape it into a ball, put it into lightly greased pans, and set aside, in a draft-free place, covered with a cloth. When the dough has again doubled in size, touch it lightly with one finger; if it feels light and springy, it is ready to bake. Bake according to the individual recipe. When the bread appears done, tap the top of the loaf with your knuckle. It should sound hollow. Turn out the bread to cool on a rack. When cool, wrap and secure well to store. All breads freeze well but should be securely wrapped twice in plastic wrap.

When making muffins, I prefer to use foil muffin tin liners. If these are not available, lightly spray the muffin tin with vegetable spray. I have found when I use paper liner, the bottom portion of the muffin sticks to the paper. I always bake Corn Bread in an iron skillet because it makes a crisp crust.

Baking Mix

Don't be caught without some in the refrigerator.

9	cups unbleached or all-purpose flour, sifted
$1/3$	cup baking powder
1	cup nonfat powdered milk
1	tablespoon salt
$1^3/4$	cups margarine

In a large bowl, combine the flour, baking powder, powdered milk, and salt. With a pastry blender or two knives, cut the margarine into mixture until the texture of cornmeal. Store in tightly sealed containers in the refrigerator.

Yield: 60 ($1/4$-cup) servings or 15 cups

1 serving contains: *Cal 92kc, Prot 2gm, Fat 3gm, Chol trace, Carb 14gm, Fib trace, Sodium 258mg*

Homemade Biscuits

Use your imagination and experiment.

Preheat the oven to 425°F (220°C). In a medium-size bowl, combine the Baking Mix and water with a fork, stirring until moistened. Turn out on a floured board and knead about 15 times. Roll out to $\frac{1}{2}$ inch thick. Cut out the biscuits with a round cutter. Place on an ungreased baking sheet. Bake for 10 minutes or until lightly browned.

2 cups Baking Mix, opposite page
$\frac{1}{2}$ cup water

Yield: 5 servings (2 biscuits each)

Variations:

+ **Cheesy Biscuits:** Before mixing ingredients, add $\frac{1}{3}$ cup reduced-fat shredded cheese.

+ **Herb Biscuits:** Before mixing ingredients, add your favorite herbs. Mix flavors to enhance your entrée.

  + **Italian**—$\frac{1}{2}$ teaspoon crushed dried leaf Italian herbs

  + **Peppy**—$\frac{1}{4}$ teaspoon dry mustard and $\frac{1}{2}$ teaspoon ground sage

  + **Chives**—$\frac{1}{4}$ cup minced chives

  + **Dill**—1 tablespoon dried dill

  + **Parsley**—1 tablespoon chopped fresh parsley

  + **Onion**—$\frac{1}{4}$ cup minced onion

1 serving contains: *Cal 154kc, Prot 4gm, Fat 4gm, Chol trace, Carb 24gm, Fib 1gm, Sodium 399mg*

Blueberry Muffins

For additional fiber substitute $1/3$ cup oat bran for $1/3$ cup flour.

$1^1/3$ cups unbleached or all-purpose flour

1 cup oats, quick or regular, uncooked

$1/4$ cup firmly packed brown sugar

1 tablespoon baking powder

$1/2$ teaspoon ground cinnamon

1 cup skim milk

2 egg whites, slightly beaten

2 tablespoons canola oil

1 cup fresh or frozen blueberries

Preheat the oven to 400°F (205°C). Line a 12-cup muffin pan with foil liners or spray a nonstick pan with vegetable spray. In a large bowl, combine the flour, oats, sugar, baking powder, and cinnamon. Add the milk, egg whites, and oil; stir until blended. Lightly fold in the blueberries. Spoon into the prepared muffin cups, filling about $2/3$ full. Bake for 25 to 30 minutes or until lightly browned. Cool for about 5 minutes before serving.

Yield: 12 servings (1 muffin each)

1 serving contains: *Cal 132kc, Prot 4gm, Fat 3gm, Chol trace, Carb 23gm, Fib 1gm, Sodium 106mg*

Oat-Bran Muffins

Begin your day with a bran muffin and a bowl of fresh fruit.

Preheat the oven to 400°F (205°C). Line a 12-cup muffin pan with foil liners or spray a nonstick pan with vegetable spray. In a medium-size bowl, combine the flour, bran, and baking powder. In a small bowl, combine the egg whites, milk, molasses, and oil. Add to the dry ingredients; stir just until well blended. Spoon into the prepared muffin cups, filling about $^2/_3$ full. Bake for 20 minutes or until lightly browned. Cool for about 5 minutes before serving.

Yield: 12 servings (1 muffin each)

$1^1/_2$	cups unbleached or all-purpose flour
1	cup oat bran
3	teaspoons baking powder
2	egg whites, slightly beaten
$^3/_4$	cup skim milk
$^1/_4$	cup molasses
3	tablespoons canola oil

Variation:

✦ Add 1 cup raisins or finely chopped apple or dates and 1 teaspoon ground cinnamon.

1 serving contains: *Cal 134kc, Prot 4gm, Fat 4gm, Chol trace, Carb 21gm, Fib 2gm, Sodium 109mg*

Cornmeal Muffins

Use fresh corn for a wonderful summer treat.

1	cup cornmeal
3/4	cup unbleached or all-purpose flour
3	tablespoons sugar
3	teaspoons baking powder
1/2	teaspoon salt
2	egg whites, slightly beaten
2/3	cup skim milk
1	cup creamed corn

Preheat the oven to 425°F (220°C). Line a 12-cup muffin pan with foil liners or spray a nonstick pan with vegetable spray. In a large bowl, combine all the dry ingredients. Add the remaining ingredients and stir until well blended. Spoon into the prepared muffin cups, filling about 2/3 full. Bake for 20 minutes or until lightly browned. Cool for about 5 minutes before removing.

Yield: 12 servings (1 muffin each)

1 serving contains: *Cal 106kc, Prot 3gm, Fat trace, Chol trace, Carb 23gm, Fib trace, Sodium 243mg*

Oatmeal Muffins

Try using chopped prunes, dates, or apricots instead of raisins.

Preheat the oven to 400°F (205°C). Line 18 muffin cups with foil liners or spray nonstick pans with vegetable spray. In a large bowl, combine the flour, sugar, baking powder, salt, cinnamon, and oats. In a small bowl, combine the oil, egg whites, and milk. Pour over the dry ingredients all at once; stir until mixed. Fold in the raisins. Do not overmix. Spoon the batter into the prepared muffin cups, filling $2/3$ full. Bake for 20 minutes or until lightly browned. Cool for about 5 minutes before serving.

Yield: 18 large muffins

1 serving contains: *Cal 170kc, Prot 5gm, Fat 4gm, Chol trace, Carb 30gm, Fib 1gm, Sodium 191mg*

2	cups unbleached or all-purpose flour
$1/2$	cup sugar
2	tablespoons baking powder
$1/2$	teaspoon salt
1	teaspoon ground cinnamon
2	cups oats, quick or regular, uncooked
$1/4$	cup canola oil
3	egg whites, slightly beaten
2	cups skim milk
1	cup raisins

Banana-Raisin Bread

A traditional bread with the added goodness of whole wheat and oat bran.

1/3	cup canola oil
1	cup firmly packed brown sugar
3	ripe bananas, mashed
1	teaspoon vanilla extract
3	egg whites, slightly beaten
1 1/2	cups whole wheat flour
1/2	cup oat bran or wheat germ
2	teaspoons baking powder
1/2	teaspoon ground cinnamon
1/2	cup raisins

Preheat the oven to 325°F (165°C). Spray a 9 x 5-inch loaf pan with vegetable spray. In a large bowl, combine the oil and sugar. Add the bananas, vanilla, and egg whites; set aside. In a medium-size bowl, combine the flour, oat bran or wheat germ, baking powder, and cinnamon. Add to the banana mixture; stir until combined. Stir in the raisins. Pour into the prepared pan. Bake for 1 hour 10 minutes or until a wooden pick comes out clean. Turn out on a rack to cool. This makes a dense loaf.

Yield: 10 servings (1 slice each)

Variation:

✦ Substitute 1 cup all-purpose flour for 1 cup whole wheat flour. Reduce sugar to 1/2 cup.

1 serving contains: *Cal 284kc, Prot 5gm, Fat 8gm, Chol 0, Carb 52gm, Fib 5gm, Sodium 92mg*

Corn Bread

Corn bread and beans is our daughter's favorite meal.

Preheat the oven to 425°F (220°C). Combine the cornmeal, flour, baking powder, and salt in a medium-size bowl. Add the milk and egg whites; stir well. Heat a 9-inch cast-iron skillet or ovenproof pan over medium-high heat. Add the oil to the skillet; while this is heating, mix the batter. Pour the batter into the hot skillet. Bake for 20 minutes or until golden brown. Serve warm.

Yield: 8 (3^1/$_2$-inch) wedges

1	cup cornmeal
1	cup unbleached or all-purpose flour
5	teaspoons baking powder
^{1}/$_2$	teaspoon salt
1	cup skim milk
2	egg whites, slightly beaten
1	teaspoon canola oil

Variation:

✦ For a sweet bread, add ^{1}/$_4$ cup sugar with the dry ingredients.

1 serving contains: *Cal 142kc, Prot 5gm, Fat 1gm, Chol 1mg, Carb 28gm, Fib trace, Sodium 363mg*

Lemon Bread

Serve with iced tea for a refreshing summer dessert or snack.

$1/2$ cup margarine, room temperature

$1^1/4$ cups sugar, divided

$1/4$ cup egg substitute (equivalent of 1 egg)

2 egg whites

$1^1/4$ cups unbleached or all-purpose flour, sifted

$1^1/2$ teaspoons baking powder

$1/4$ teaspoon salt

$1/2$ cup skim milk

3 teaspoons grated lemon peel

3 tablespoons fresh lemon juice

Preheat the oven to 350°F (175°C). Spray a 9 x 5-inch loaf pan with vegetable spray. In a large bowl, beat the margarine and 1 cup of the sugar until light and fluffy. In a small bowl, beat the egg substitute and egg whites together. Add to the sugar mixture. Sift the flour, baking powder, and salt into a medium-size bowl. Add to the sugar mixture, alternating the dry ingredients with the milk; mix well. Stir in the lemon peel. Pour into the prepared pan. Bake for 1 hour or until a wooden pick comes out clean. In a small bowl, combine the remaining $1/4$ cup sugar and lemon juice; stir until the sugar is dissolved. Drizzle over the warm bread while still in the pan. Let stand for 5 minutes, then invert onto a cake rack; remove the pan and turn the bread right side up. Let cool before slicing.

Yield: 10 servings (1 slice each)

1 serving contains: *Cal 197kc, Prot 3gm, Fat 5gm, Chol trace, Carb 36gm, Fib trace, Sodium 238mg*

Mexican Corn Bread

Great served with a hearty bean soup or chili.

Preheat the oven to 425°F (220°C). Lay the green chilies on paper towels to drain. In a large bowl, combine the flour, 1 cup cornmeal, baking powder, salt, and sugar. Add the egg whites and milk; stir. Add the creamed corn and chilies; stir. The batter should be thin enough to pour into the skillet, but not runny. Add more milk if needed for pouring consistency. Heat the oil in a 9-inch iron skillet or ovenproof pan. Sprinkle 1 teaspoon cornmeal into the hot skillet and heat just a few seconds until the cornmeal is lightly browned. Pour the batter into the skillet. Bake for 30 minutes or until lightly browned. Invert onto a round 10-inch heatproof serving plate. Serve warm.

Yield: 8 (3$^{1}/_{2}$-inch) wedges

1 serving contains: *Cal 123kc, Prot 4gm, Fat 1gm, Chol trace, Carb 25 gm, Fib trace, Sodium 439mg*

$^{1}/_{4}$	cup diced green chilies, drained
1	cup unbleached or all-purpose flour
1	cup plus 1 teaspoon cornmeal, divided
4	teaspoons baking powder
$^{1}/_{2}$	teaspoon salt
1	tablespoon sugar
2	egg whites, slightly beaten
$^{2}/_{3}$	cup milk
1	cup creamed corn
1	teaspoon canola oil

Whole Wheat Molasses Bread

Great for luncheon sandwiches.

Cornmeal, if desired

$1/2$ cup molasses

1 cup skim milk

$1/4$ cup unbleached or all-purpose flour

2 cups whole wheat flour

$1/2$ cup sugar

1 teaspoon baking soda

$1/4$ teaspoon salt

Preheat the oven to 350°F (175°C). Lightly oil a 9 x 5-inch loaf pan or spray with vegetable spray; sprinkle with the cornmeal, if desired. In a medium-size bowl, combine the molasses and milk. In another medium-size bowl, combine the flours, sugar, baking soda, and salt. Add to the molasses and milk; stir until well mixed. Pour into a loaf pan. Bake for 1 hour or until a wooden pick comes out clean. Invert onto a rack and cool.

Yield: 10 slices (1 slice per serving)

1 serving contains: *Cal 172kc, Prot 4gm, Fat trace, Chol trace, Carb 39gm, Fib 3gm, Sodium 159mg*

Dilly Bread

Dill gives it that tantalizing flavor.

In a small bowl, dissolve the yeast in the warm water; set aside. In a large bowl, combine the cottage cheese, sugar, onion, margarine, dill weed, salt, and baking soda. Add the egg whites to yeast mixture; mix well. Add to the cottage cheese mixture, blending well. If you have mixer with a dough hook, use it. If not, mix and knead dough by hand on a floured board. Gradually add the flour and beat until dough pulls away from bowl, about 5 minutes, or knead by hand on a floured board. Place in a greased bowl. Cover and let rise in a warm place until doubled in bulk. Preheat the oven to 350°F (175°C). Spray a shallow round 2-quart casserole with vegetable spray; dust with cornmeal. When the dough has doubled, punch down and knead again a few times. Put in prepared casserole. Let rise again until doubled. Bake for 40 to 50 minutes or until lightly browned. Remove from pan. Cool before slicing.

Yield: 12 servings (1 slice each)

1 serving contains: *Cal 126kc, Prot 6gm, Fat 1gm, Chol 1mg, Carb 23gm, Fib 1gm, Sodium 277mg*

1	($1/4$-ounce) package dry yeast, about 1 tablespoon
$1/4$	cup warm water (110°F, 45°C)
1	cup reduced-fat, small-curd cottage cheese, room temperature
2	tablespoons sugar
2	tablespoons minced onion
1	tablespoon margarine, room temperature
2	teaspoons dill weed
1	teaspoon salt
$1/4$	teaspoon baking soda
2	egg whites, slightly beaten
$2^{1}/2$	cups unbleached or all-purpose flour
1	teaspoon cornmeal

Honey Whole Wheat Bread

My own blue ribbon recipe.

2	cups whole wheat flour
1	cup nonfat powdered milk
3	($1/4$-ounce) packages active dry yeast, about 3 tablespoons
1	tablespoon salt
2	cups warm water (110°F, 45°C)
$1/3$	cup canola oil
$1/3$	cup honey
5 to 6 cups unbleached or all-purpose flour, divided
Cornmeal, if desired

In a bowl, combine the wheat flour, powdered milk, yeast, and salt. Add all liquids and mix well. Stir in 4 cups unbleached or all-purpose flour. If you have a dough hook, use it. If not, mix and knead by hand. Add the remaining flour, $1/2$ cup at a time, until the dough clings to the hook and cleans the side of the bowl. Knead for 7 to 10 minutes, until smooth and elastic. Add flour if necessary to keep sides of bowl clean. Make an indentation with you finger in the dough; it will spring back if it is kneaded enough. Place in a lightly oiled bowl. Cover with a cloth and let rise until doubled in bulk. Press your finger lightly into the dough. If indentation remains, the dough is ready. Lightly oil three (9 x 5-inch) loaf pans; sprinkle with cornmeal, if desired. Punch the dough down and turn it out onto a lightly floured board; knead for 1 or 2 minutes. Divide the dough in half and shape into loaves. Place in prepared loaf pans; cover with a cloth. Let rise again until doubled. Preheat the oven to 375°F (190°C). Bake for 20 to 25 minutes or until golden brown. Cool before slicing.

Yield: 15 servings (2 slices each)

1 serving contains: *Cal 306kc, Prot 9gm, Fat 5gm, Chol 1mg, Carb 55gm, Fib 3gm, Sodium 418mg*

Jean's Italian Bread

For added flavor, sprinkle with 3 to 4 tablespoons chopped herbs after dough is rolled into a rectangle.

Lightly oil a large bowl. In another bowl, combine the yeast, salt, sugar, and 2 cups flour; stir to blend. Add the water and mix. Stir in 2 more cups flour. Put in the mixer with a dough hook. If kneading by hand, knead until smooth and elastic. Gradually add the remaining flour, 1/2 cup at a time as needed. Mix until the dough clings to hook and cleans the sides of bowl. Continue kneading for 5 minutes. Place the dough in a prepared bowl. Make a slight indentation on the top and pour the margarine over the top. Spread over all. Cover and let rise until doubled. Spray a cookie sheet with vegetable spray. On a floured surface, punch down the dough and divide it into two equal parts. Roll each half into a rectangle, then roll up jelly-roll fashion. Place on the prepared cookie sheet, seam side down. Set in a cold oven for 30 minutes. Leaving bread in oven, set oven to 400°F (205°C) and bake for 30 minutes or until lightly browned. Cool before slicing.

Yield: 15 servings (2 slices per serving) or 2 loaves

1 serving contains: *Cal 176kc, Prot 5gm, Fat 1gm, Chol 0, Carb 36gm, Fib 1gm, Sodium 401mg,*

2 (1/4-ounce) packages active dry yeast, about 2 tablespoons

1 tablespoon salt

1 tablespoon sugar

5 to 6 cups unbleached or all-purpose flour, divided

2 cups warm water (110°F, 45°C)

1 tablespoon margarine or butter, melted

Note: You can make focaccia by shaping dough into an 11 x 14-inch greased baking sheet. Drizzle with oil, sprinkle with Italian herbs. Bake at 475°F for about 12 minutes. You can also use this dough as pizza dough.

Hot Garlic Bread

Great accompaniment for your favorite Italian dish.

3 tablespoons margarine, room temperature

$1/2$ teaspoon parsley flakes

$1/8$ teaspoon ground oregano

$1/8$ teaspoon dill weed

$1/8$ teaspoon garlic powder

1 (1-pound) loaf Italian bread

1 tablespoon grated Parmesan cheese

Preheat the oven to 400°F (205°C). In a small bowl, blend the margarine, parsley, oregano, dill, and garlic powder. Slice the bread and spread the herb mixture on one side of each slice. Reassemble the slices forming a loaf. Place on a large sheet of aluminum foil. Fold the foil over the sides, leaving the top open (shape like a boat). Sprinkle the Parmesan cheese over bread. Bake for 10 minutes or until lightly browned. Serve hot.

Yield: 20 slices

1 serving contains: *Cal 73kc, Prot 2gm, Fat 1gm, Chol trace, Carb 13gm, Fib trace, Sodium 142mg*

How to Shape Rolls

Parkerhouse Rolls: Place dough on a floured board and roll out until about ¼-inch thick. Cut out with a biscuit cutter. Fold across so top half slightly overlaps bottom. Press edges together at fold. Place on an ungreased baking sheet.

Dinner Rolls: Pinch off dough and roll into balls about ⅓ the size desired. Place on an ungreased baking sheet; do not let rolls touch.

Soft Dinner Rolls: Pinch off dough and roll into balls about ⅓ the size desired. Place close together in a lightly oiled round pan.

Cloverleaf Rolls: Pinch off dough and roll into balls about 1 inch in diameter. Place 3 balls in each lightly greased muffin cup.

Crescent Rolls: Pinch off dough and roll into a cylindrical shape, tapering at each end. Place on an ungreased baking sheet and lightly shape dough into a crescent shape.

After shaping, all rolls need to rise until doubled in size. Bake at 400°F (205°C) for 12 to 15 minutes or until lightly browned.

Dinner Rolls

Always a holiday treat when I was growing up.

2	($1/4$-ounce) packages active dry yeast, about 2 tablespoons
$1/2$	cup warm water (110°F, 45°C)
$1^3/4$	cups skim milk, lukewarm
$1/4$	cup margarine or butter, melted
$1/4$	cup sugar
$1/2$	tablespoon salt
6	cups or more unbleached or all-purpose flour, divided

In a large mixing bowl, dissolve yeast in water. Add the milk, margarine, sugar, salt, and 4 cups flour. In you have a dough hook, use it. If not, mix and knead the dough by hand. Add 2 cups flour, $1/2$ cup at a time, until the dough clings to the hook and cleans the sides of the bowl. When the dough is smooth and elastic, place in a large lightly oiled bowl; cover with a cloth. Let rise in a warm place until doubled, about 1 hour. Press your finger into the dough; if indentation remains, the dough is ready. Punch down the dough and let it rise again until almost doubled, about 30 minutes. Spray a baking sheet with vegetable spray. Shape into rolls and place on the prepared baking sheet. Cover and let rise until doubled, about 25 minutes. Preheat the oven to 400°F (205°C). Bake for 12 to 15 minutes or until golden brown.

Yield: 48 rolls

1 roll contains: *Cal 69kc, Prot 2gm, Fat 1gm, Chol trace, Carb 13gm, Fib trace, Sodium 78mg*

Cinnamon Rolls

Yummy Cinnamon rolls without the usual fat. Glaze with your favorite icing.

Combine the sugar and cinnamon; set aside. After the dough for Dinner Rolls has risen the second time, divide into 2 sections. Roll 1 section into a rectangle about 12 x 9 inches. Spread with 1 tablespoon margarine and half of the cinnamon sugar. Scatter half of the raisins over all. Tightly roll up the dough, beginning at the wide side. Seal the edges by pinching together. Cut the roll into 1-inch slices. Spray a round 8-inch pan with vegetable spray. Place the dough slices in the pan. Repeat for the second half of the dough. Cover and let rise about 45 minutes until doubled in bulk. Preheat the oven to 350°F (175°C). Bake the rolls for 15 minutes or until lightly brown. Invert pan onto a plate; let stand 5 minutes before removing pan. Serve warm.

Yield: 16 rolls

$3/4$	cup sugar
3	teaspoons ground cinnamon
$1/2$	recipe for Dinner Rolls, opposite page
2	tablespoons margarine or butter, room temperature
$1 1/2$	cups raisins, divided

1 roll without icing contains: *Cal 184kc, Prot 4gm, Fat 2gm, Chol trace, Carb 40gm, Fib 2gm, Sodium 135mg*

Pancakes

Vary these pancakes by adding $1/2$ cup raisins or blueberries.

3   egg whites, slightly
    beaten

2   cups Baking Mix,
    page 66

About $1^1/4$ cups skim milk,
divided

$1/8$ teaspoon canola oil

In a medium-size bowl, combine the egg whites, Baking Mix, and 1 cup milk. Using a wire whisk or fork, mix just until blended; do not beat. Add the remaining milk if needed to keep the batter thin enough to pour. Pour the oil into a nonstick griddle or skillet. Using a paper towel, spread oil around. Heat the griddle over medium-high heat. Pour about $1/4$ cup batter onto the griddle (use more or less batter according to your personal preference for thickness). Cook until the pancake is covered with bubbles; turn and cook until lightly browned. Serve immediately.

Yield: 10 ($5^1/2$-inch) pancakes

1 pancake contains: *Cal 75kc, Prot 4gm, Fat trace, Chol 1mg, Carb 14gm, Fib trace, Sodium 180mg*

Basic Crêpe Batter

Enjoy these no-cholesterol crêpes filled with chicken.

Combine the egg whites and egg substitute in a mixing bowl. In a separate bowl, combine the flour, salt, and powdered milk. Add the dry mixture alternately with water to the eggs; beat until smooth. Cover and refrigerate for at least 1 hour. Heat a nonstick crêpe pan over medium heat. Brush a drop of oil around the pan. Using a scoop or cup equivalent to 3 tablespoons, pour the batter into the pan. Immediately tilt the pan, swirling the batter to cover evenly the bottom of the pan. Cook until the bottom is brown and the top appears dry. It is not necessary to cook the other side. Stack the cooked crêpes on a plate. When the crêpes are cooked, fill or store for later use. If you plan to refrigerate or freeze the crêpes, place waxed paper or foil between each one and wrap. Store in an airtight container.

2	egg whites
$1/2$	cup egg substitute (or the equivalent of 2 eggs)
1	cup unbleached or all-purpose flour
$1/8$	teaspoon salt
2	tablespoons nonfat powdered milk
1	cup water

Yield: 15 crêpes

Variation:

✦ **Dessert Crêpes:** To the above recipe add 2 tablespoons sugar, 1 tablespoon nonfat powdered milk, and 1 teaspoon vanilla extract.

1 crêpe contains: *Cal 42kc, Prot 3gm, Fat trace, Chol trace, Carb 7gm, Fib trace, Sodium 40mg*

85

French Toast with Steamed Apples

A perfect brunch dish. Prepare ahead and arrange in a chafing dish to keep warm.

2 egg whites

1/2 cup egg substitute (or the equivalent of 2 eggs)

2/3 cup skim milk

1 tablespoon nonfat powdered milk

8 slices French bread, 3/4-inch thick

2 red cooking apples, cored, sliced

1/2 tablespoon water

1/2 cup raisins

1 teaspoon canola oil, divided

3 tablespoons powdered sugar

In a medium-size bowl, combine the egg whites, egg substitute, milk, and powdered milk. Pour into a 13 x 9-inch pan. Place the bread slices in the egg mixture for 10 minutes; turn carefully. Let stand until the liquid is absorbed. In a nonstick skillet over low heat, add the apple slices and water. Cover and cook for 10 minutes or until tender. Add the raisins; cover and set aside. While the apples are cooking, spray a large nonstick skillet with vegetable spray and heat over medium heat. Brush with 1/2 teaspoon oil. Gently lift 4 bread slices into the skillet. Cook until lightly browned; turn and cook the remaining side for 4 to 5 minutes or until lightly browned. Repeat with the remaining oil and bread. Arrange the toast on a serving plate. Top with apples and raisins; sift powdered sugar over all. Serve immediately.

Yield: 4 servings (2 slices each)

1 serving contains: *Cal 371kc, Prot 15gm, Fat 5gm, Chol 1mg, Carb 68gm, Fib 4gm, Sodium 499mg*

Salads

Salads can be the most versatile part of your menu. A dish like Chicken Pasta Salad can be served as a lunch or supper main course, with Tomato-Onion Soup contributing a texture and color contrast as the side dish. Follow this with refreshing Fresh Fruit Salad, and you will have given your guests a well-rounded and attractive meal. Provide the little bit of extra "body" such a menu may require by offering delicious home-baked breads or rolls from your own oven or a local bakery.

The only caution when planning a meal composed mainly of salads is to make sure foods are combined with a variety of dressings. If all your salads have a vinaigrette or mayonnaise-type dressing, there will be a sameness to the dishes no matter what the actual composition of the salad. A salad buffet is such a natural for summer entertaining, so it is worth looking for unusual dressing and sauce recipes throughout the year.

This section includes a wide variety of salads chosen for their nutritional value as well as taste and eye appeal.

Always make your salad with the freshest ingredients possible. The success of a tossed salad depends on the crispness of the greens and the freshness of other vegetables. The same holds true for fruit salads. How often have you been disappointed in the flavor of a basket of color-perfect strawberries once you get them home from the supermarket? Appearance is not always a guarantee with fruit. You may have to pay extra at a specialty produce market to get the best flavor and texture.

Carefully wash vegetables or fruit thoroughly with cold water. Drain in a colander, then on paper towels. When fairly dry, put in a plastic bag or plastic container and refrigerate. I don't wash my ingredients until the day I plan to use them.

Tossed salads can be made several hours ahead. Tear the lettuce instead of cutting it. Place all ingredients, except tomato, into a large bowl, and cover with a slightly damp cotton cloth until ready to serve.

Fresh fruit can be prepared ahead but must be treated with an ascorbic acid mixture, such as Fruit Fresh, or by dipping the cut fruit into lemon juice to prevent it from turning brown.

Many salads are quick and easy to put together if you keep a variety of greens and other vegetables in the refrigerator. For an attractive, simple spinach salad, tear washed and dried spinach leaves and place on a salad plate. Garnish with tomato wedges and overlap a few red onion rings on top of the spinach. Sprinkle a few toasted croutons over all and serve with Creamy Dressing, page 119.

The increased availability of reduced-fat cheeses and dressings makes it possible to enjoy your salad favorites like chef's salad. Plain reduced-fat yogurt can usually be substituted successfully for part of the mayonnaise or sour cream in a creamy dressing or use the reduced-fat version.

Try livening up a cottage cheese–stuffed tomato with a sprinkling of chopped fresh herbs. These are available in many markets today and may go a long way toward making diet restrictions palatable. Another easy cottage cheese idea is to use pears or peaches, canned in "lite" syrup, as the base. Spoon cottage cheese into a hollow of the fruit and top with chopped fresh mint.

To help you serve your family at least one salad course a day, here is a list of unusual and tasty salad ingredients. Use any of them together or combine with old favorites.

Artichoke hearts, not packed in oil
Asparagus, cooked
Bell peppers, roasted or raw
Broccoli
Cauliflower
Mushrooms, sliced or whole
Peas, fresh or frozen
Sprouts
Sugar snap peas
Summer squash
Water chestnuts
Zucchini

To roast bell or chile peppers, preheat oven to broil. Place peppers on a baking pan. Broil until skin blisters and starts to turn black, turning a few times to cook evenly. Place peppers in a paper bag, close bag and let stand a few minutes. Remove peppers from bag and peel off skin. These make a delicious addition to any salad or serve them alone with a simple vinaigrette dressing. You may want to protect your hands with rubber gloves when working with chiles.

Fresh Fruit Salad

Use any combination of fruit. Add honey dressing when the fruit is not very flavorful; otherwise enjoy the fresh natural taste alone.

In a medium-size bowl, combine the fruit. In a small bowl, blend the honey and lemon juice; drizzle over the fruit and toss gently to coat. Sprinkle with walnuts before serving.

Yield: About 10 (^{1}/$_2$-cup) servings

Variation:

✦ **Cottage Cheese and Fresh Fruit Salad:** Spoon fruit into individual lettuce-lined serving dishes. Top fruit with ^{1}/$_3$ cup reduced-fat cottage cheese and garnish with sliced fresh strawberries.

1 serving contains: *Cal 49kc, Prot 1gm, Fat 1g, Chol 0, Carb 11gm, Fib 1gm, Sodium 3mg*

^{1}/$_2$ cantaloupe, cut into bite-size pieces
2 peaches, sliced
1 banana, cubed
2 tablespoons honey
^{1}/$_2$ teaspoon lemon juice
2 tablespoons chopped walnuts

Green Salad with Fresh Pears, Feta, and Raspberry Vinaigrette

This combination gives your salad a nice change.

2 tablespoons sugar

1 tablespoon raspberry vinegar or white wine vinegar

2 tablespoons canola or extra-virgin olive oil

1 teaspoon minced onion

4 cups loosely packed salad greens

2 ripe pears*

1/4 cup crumbled Feta cheese

1 tablespoon sliced almonds, toasted

Combine the sugar and vinegar in a medium mixing bowl; slowly add the olive oil, beating constantly with a whisk until well blended and the oil is emulsified; add onion and stir.

Place the salad greens in a large salad bowl; remove the seeds from the pears and slice, dip the pears in a mixture of Fruit Fresh or lemon juice to prevent browning. Arrange the pears over the greens and sprinkle cheese over all. Slowly drizzle dressing over all and toss gently. Sprinkle with almonds and serve immediately.

Yield: 4 servings

* If you are not going to serve immediately, treat sliced pears with a mixture of Fruit Fresh or lemon juice to keep from turning brown.

Note: **This is especially attractive when using red-skinned pears.**

1 serving contains: *Cal 173kc, Prot 4gm, Fat 9gm, Chol 3mg, Carb 22gm, Fib 4gm, Sodium 145mg*

Special Occasion Three-Bean Salad

A great dish for potlucks.

In a large bowl, combine all the ingredients, tossing gently to coat all the vegetables. Cover and refrigerate for several hours or overnight. To serve, spoon the salad into an attractive serving bowl.

Yield: 12 (^{1}/2-cup) servings

1 serving contains: *Cal 116kc, Prot 4gm, Fat 6gm, Chol 0, Carb 12gm, Fib 3gm, Sodium 152mg*

1^1/2	cups cooked white beans, drained
1^1/2	cups cooked kidney beans, drained
1^1/2	cups cooked green beans, drained
^{1}/3	cup finely diced celery
^{1}/3	cup sliced green onion
^{1}/3	cup canola oil
2	tablespoons wine vinegar
1	teaspoon Italian seasoning
^{1}/2	teaspoon dried leaf tarragon
3	packages artificial sweetener, optional

Coleslaw

Like my mom used to make! Bell pepper rings make an attractive garnish.

3 cups shredded cabbage

1 small carrot, shredded

$^1/_2$ teaspoon vinegar

1 tablespoon sugar

2 tablespoons skim milk

$^1/_3$ cup reduced-fat mayonnaise

Dash of pepper

Red or green bell pepper rings, optional

In a medium-size bowl, combine the cabbage and carrot. In a small bowl, mix the vinegar, sugar, milk, mayonnaise, and pepper. Pour over the cabbage and toss gently until well coated. Refrigerate for 2 to 3 hours until ready to serve. To serve, transfer the coleslaw to a serving bowl.

Yield: 6 ($^1/_2$-cup) servings

1 serving contains: *Cal 43kc, Prot 1gm, Fat 2gm, Chol 2mg, Carb 8gm, Fib 1gm, Sodium 54mg*

Marinated Cucumbers

Make this sweet-tart salad the day before you serve it. For additional color and texture, add pimiento strips and alfalfa sprouts just before serving.

In a small saucepan, bring the vinegar, water, sweetener, salt, and pepper to a boil. Reduce the heat and simmer for about 10 minutes; cool. Pour the marinade over the cucumbers in a serving bowl. Sprinkle with the dill. Refrigerate for several hours before serving.

Yield: 4 (^{1}/2-cup) servings

1 serving contains: *Cal 13kc, Prot trace, Fat trace, Chol 0, Carb 4gm, Fib 1gm, Sodium 4mg*

^{1}/2 cup vinegar

2 tablespoons water

2 packages artificial sweetener

Salt and pepper to taste

2 medium-size cucumbers, thinly sliced

^{1}/2 teaspoon dill weed

Tuna-Rice Salad

Ideal for a light, cool summer luncheon. Add sugar peas and cherry tomatoes for an attractive edible garnish.

1   (6$^1/_2$-ounce) can white tuna, packed in water

2   cups cooked long-grain rice

1   cup peas, cooked

$^1/_2$ cup diced reduced-fat Swiss cheese

1   tablespoon chopped fresh parsley

$^1/_2$ cup reduced-fat mayonnaise

$^1/_2$ teaspoon dry mustard

$^1/_2$ teaspoon wine vinegar

$^1/_4$ teaspoon pepper

Leaf lettuce

Drain the tuna well; place in a medium-size bowl. Break apart the tuna with a fork. Add the rice, peas, cheese, and parsley. In a small bowl, blend the mayonnaise, mustard, vinegar, and pepper. Pour over the tuna mixture, tossing gently to mix well. To serve, arrange on a lettuce-lined platter.

Yield: 4 (1-cup) servings

1 serving contains: *Cal 272kc, Prot 21gm, Fat 7gm, Chol 28mg, Carb 35gm, Fib 3gm, Sodium 311mg*

Tuna Salad

Use for tuna salad sandwiches—an old favorite for lunch.

Drain the tuna well; place in a small bowl. Break apart the tuna with a fork. Peel the egg and discard the yolk; dice the white. Add the mayonnaise, celery, relish, and egg white; toss gently to combine. Use as desired.

Yield: 2 (^{1}/$_2$-cup) servings

1	(6^1/$_2$-ounce) can white tuna, packed in water
1	hard-boiled egg
2	tablespoons reduced-fat mayonnaise
1	tablespoon finely chopped celery
1	tablespoon pickle relish

Serving Suggestions:

✦ Use to stuff fresh tomatoes, then serve on a bed of spinach with alfalfa sprouts.

✦ Boil eggs; discard yolk. Stuff egg centers with tuna salad and arrange on a bed of greens. Garnish with cherry tomatoes.

✦ Add chopped apple for a nice crunch.

1 serving contains: *Cal 157kc, Prot 28gm, Fat 4gm, Chol 34mg, Carb 5gm, Fib trace, Sodium 469mg*

Tropical Tuna Salad

A fun and easy nutritious lunch.

1   (20-ounce) can
    pineapple chunks,
    packed in natural juice,
    drained

2   (6^1/2-ounce) cans white
    tuna, packed in water,
    flaked

^{1}/2 cup coarsely chopped red
    bell pepper

2   tablespoons chopped
    pimientos

^{1}/2 cup reduced-fat
    mayonnaise

2   bananas, sliced

1   medium-size head
    lettuce, washed,
    drained

In a large bowl, combine the pineapple, tuna, bell pepper, pimientos, and mayonnaise. Toss gently to mix, then refrigerate for 2 to 3 hours or until ready to serve. To serve, add the sliced bananas and toss gently to mix. Cut the head of lettuce into 6 wedges. Lay each wedge on a luncheon plate and spoon the tuna salad alongside the lettuce.

Yield: 6 (1-cup) servings

1 serving contains: *Cal 187kc, Prot 19mg, Fat 4gm, Chol 24mg, Carb 22gm, Fib 2gm, Sodium 291mg*

Spinach-Apple Salad

Yummy combination with lots of fiber.

Place the spinach, apple, celery, and dried cherries in a salad bowl. In a small bowl combine the vinegar and sugar; slowly add the olive oil, beating constantly with a whisk until well blended and the oil is emulsified. Pour over the salad and toss gently. Serve immediately.

Yield: 8 servings

*Fuji, cameo, etc.

1 serving contains: *Cal 114kc, Prot 3gm, Fat 7gm, Chol 0, Carb 12gm, Fib 4gm, Sodium 85mg*

16 ounces spinach, washed and torn

1 large crunchy apple*, chopped

1/4 cup thinly sliced celery

1/4 cup dried cherries, dried cranberries, or gold raisins

2 tablespoons white balsamic vinegar

2 teaspoons sugar

1/4 cup extra-virgin olive oil

Cabbage Salad

Perfect salad for a crowd.

2	teaspoons all-purpose flour
1^1/$_2$	cups sugar
1	cup vinegar
1	tablespoon margarine
^{1}/$_2$	tablespoon ground turmeric
1	teaspoon salt
1	medium head cabbage, shredded, about 7 cups
^{3}/$_4$	cup finely chopped red and/or green bell pepper
^{3}/$_4$	cup finely chopped onion
1	cup finely chopped celery

In a large saucepan, combine the flour and sugar; add the vinegar and margarine. Stir over medium heat until the sugar is dissolved. Add the turmeric, salt, cabbage, bell pepper, onion, and celery. Heat through, stirring constantly; do not boil. Cool, then cover and refrigerate at least overnight before serving. This salad will keep well for several days.

Yield: 11 (1-cup) servings

1 serving contains: *Cal 129kc, Prot 1gm, Fat 1gm, Chol 0, Carb 33gm, Fib 2gm, Sodium 212mg*

Frozen Cabbage Salad

Keep several containers in the freezer.

In a large bowl, place the shredded cabbage and sprinkle with the salt; let stand for 1 hour. Drain well. Add the bell pepper and celery; toss gently. In a medium-size saucepan, combine the sugar, vinegar, water, cloves, mustard seed, and celery seed. Bring to a boil and boil for 1 minute. Immediately pour over the cabbage mixture. Pack in sterile freezer containers, making sure the syrup covers the top of the cabbage; freeze for up to 6 months. Thaw in the refrigerator as needed. This salad will keep for several days in the refrigerator.

Yield: 18 (^{1}/2-cup) servings

1 serving contains: *Cal 135k, Prot 1gm, Fat trace, Chol 0, Carb 36gm, Fib 1gm, Sodium 175mg*

1	medium head of cabbage, finely shredded, about 7 cups
^{1}/2	tablespoon salt
^{3}/4	cup chopped red and/or green bell pepper
^{3}/4	cup chopped celery
3	cups sugar
1^1/2	cups vinegar
^{3}/4	cup water
^{1}/4	teaspoon ground cloves
1^1/2	teaspoons mustard seed
1^1/2	teaspoons celery seed

Carolyn's Cauliflower Salad

Always a favorite at luncheons.

4 cups cauliflowerets

1/2 cup diced onion

1 cup reduced-fat mayonnaise

1/2 cup shredded reduced-fat Cheddar cheese

1/3 cup imitation bacon bits (no fat)

In a clear glass bowl, layer the cauliflowerets and onion. Carefully spread the mayonnsaise over the vegetables. Sprinkle the cheese, then bacon bits over the vegetables. Cover and refrigerate overnight for the flavors to blend. Before serving, toss to mix.

Yield: 10 (1/2-cup) servings

1 serving contains: *Cal 83kc, Prot 4gm, Fat 1gm, Chol 7mg, Carb 8gm, Fib 1gm, Sodium 200mg*

Cranberry-Orange Salad

Delicious for holidays or any day.

Drain the oranges well, reserving the juice. Set aside the juice and oranges.

In a small saucepan, mix the gelatin and sugar; stir in the juice from the oranges. Stir over low heat until dissolved. Transfer to a bowl and refrigerate. When the gelatin mixture begins to set, stir in the cranberry sauce, oranges, and celery. Spoon into a serving container. Refrigerate for several hours or until firm.

Yield: 6 (^{1}/$_2$-cup) servings

1   (11-ounce) can mandarin oranges with juice
1   package unflavored gelatin
2   tablespoons sugar
1   (16-ounce) can whole cranberry sauce
^{1}/$_2$ cup finely chopped celery

Variation:

✦ If your diet allows, add ¼ cup finely chopped nuts with oranges.

Serving Suggestion:

✦ Salad can be made in a decorative mold, individual molds, or a loaf pan, then unmolded onto a bed of lettuce.

1 serving contains: *Cal 148kc, Prot 1gm, Fat trace, Chol 0, Carb 35gm, Fib 1gm, Sodium 34mg*

Sparkling Fruit Cup

A colorful, sparkling summer salad.

1   cup honeydew melon
    balls or bite-size pieces

1   cup watermelon balls
    or bite-size pieces

1   cup Bing cherries,
    pitted

1   cup grapes

1   tablespoon snipped fresh
    mint

1   cup lemon-lime
    carbonated beverage

In a medium bowl, combine the fruit and mint; refrigerate until ready to serve. Immediately before serving, spoon the fruit mixture into individual dishes. Slowly pour the lemon-lime beverage over the fruit.

Yield: 8 ($^1/_2$-cup) servings

Note: Mango, pineapple, and raspberry is a great combination also.

1 serving contains: *Cal 40kc, Prot trace, Fat trace, Chol 0, Carb 10gm, Fib 1gm, Sodium 5mg*

Macaroni Salad

Perfect dish for a patio party.

Cook the macaroni according to package directions; drain. Peel the eggs and discard the yolks; dice the whites. In a large bowl, combine the macaroni, egg whites, green onion, celery, pickles, pimiento, salt, and pepper; set aside.

To make the dressing, combine the sugar, vinegar, mustard, and mayonnaise in a small bowl; stir well to blend. Pour the dressing over the salad. Cover and refrigerate until chilled. When ready to serve, lightly dust with paprika.

Yield: 14 (^{1}/$_2$-cup) servings

1 serving contains: *Cal 74kc, Prot 2gm, Fat 2gm, Chol 2 mg, Carb 13gm, Fib trace, Sodium 213mg*

2	cups elbow macaroni
4	hard-boiled eggs
^{1}/$_3$	cup sliced green onion
^{1}/$_3$	cup diced celery
^{1}/$_3$	cup chopped dill pickles
1	(4-ounce) jar pimiento
^{1}/$_2$	teaspoon salt
^{1}/$_4$	teaspoon pepper
Dash of paprika	

Dressing:

3	tablespoons sugar
1	teaspoon cider vinegar
2	teaspoons yellow mustard
1	cup reduced-fat mayonnaise

Broccoli-Chicken Salad

4 boneless, skinless
chicken breast halves*

1/2 cup white wine

Dash white Worcestershire
sauce

6 ounces chutney**

1/2 cup reduced-fat
mayonnaise

4 cups fresh broccoli
florettes

5 green onions,
thinly sliced

1/2 cup dried cranberries
(or raisins)

Preheat the oven to 350°F (175°C). Coat a 9 x 9-inch casserole with vegetable spray. Rinse the chicken and pat dry; place the chicken in the prepared baking dish. Combine the wine and Worcestershire sauce; pour over the chicken. Cover and bake for 45 to 50 minutes or until tender. Drain, cool, and cut into bite-size pieces; set aside.

While the chicken is cooking, combine the chutney and mayonnaise; refrigerate until ready to use. Combine the broccoli, green onions, cranberries, and chicken; spoon the mayonnaise mixture over all, tossing gently to coat. Cover; refrigerate until ready to serve.

Yield: 8 servings

* You can use rotisserie chicken from the market if preferred.

** I like to use pineapple/mango chutney or Major Grey chutney.

Note: **For an attractive presentation, line a serving platter or bowl with lettuce leaves, spoon salad over lettuce and serve.**

1 serving contains: *Cal 236kc, Prot 19gm, Fat 8gm, Chol 53mg, Carb 21gm, Fib 1gm, Sodium 217*

Sylvia's Orange-Gelatin Salad

Carrots and pineapple make this salad high in vitamin A.

In a large bowl, combine the gelatin with the boiling water, stirring until the gelatin is dissolved. Stir in the cold water, pineapple, and pineapple juice. Refrigerate until the gelatin starts to set. Add the raisins and carrot. Pour into a shallow 9-inch square dish. Refrigerate for several hours or overnight until gelatin is firm.

Yield: 9 ($1/2$-cup) servings

1 serving contains: *Cal 43kc, Prot 1gm, Fat trace, Chol 0, Carb 9gm, Fib 1gm, Sodium 58mg*

1	(16-ounce) package sugar-free orange gelatin
2	cups boiling water
1	cup cold water
1	(8-ounce) can crushed pineapple, packed in natural juice, not drained
$1/2$	cup golden raisins
$3/4$	cup shredded carrot

Pasta Primavera

Variety of vegetables makes a colorful, nutritious salad.

2 cups macaroni or your favorite pasta

1/2 tablespoon extra-virgin olive oil

1 garlic clove, minced

2 cups raw vegetables, cut for stir-frying

About 1 cup oil-free Italian salad dressing

Cherry tomatoes for garnish

Cook the macaroni according to package directions; drain. In a wok or large nonstick skillet, heat the oil until it sizzles. Stir the garlic in the oil for 3 or 4 seconds, then add the vegetables. Stir-fry for 1 to 2 minutes on high heat, then reduce the heat to medium high. Cook for 1 to 2 minutes longer or until crisp-tender. Place the macaroni in a large serving bowl; add the stir-fried vegetables. Pour the salad dressing over all, tossing gently to coat all pieces well. Refrigerate for 2 to 6 hours until ready to serve. It may be necessary to add more dressing before serving. To serve, garnish with cherry tomatoes.

Yield: Approximately 8 (1-cup) servings

Suggested vegetables for stir-frying:

+ Broccoli   + Green bell pepper

+ Carrots   + Onion

+ Cauliflower   + Zucchini

1 serving contains: *Cal 145kc, Prot 4gm, Fat 4gm, Chol 2mg, Carb 23mg, Fib 1gm, Sodium 243mg*

Pickled Beets and Onions

A crunchy, colorful side dish.

In a medium saucepan, combine the vinegar, water, beet juice, sugar or sweetener, and pickling spice. Bring to a boil; reduce the heat and simmer for about 10 minutes. Strain and cool. Pour over the beets and onions in a medium bowl. Refrigerate for several hours before serving.

Yield: 8 (1/2-cup) servings

1 serving contains: *Cal 39kc, Prot 1gm, Fat trace, Chol 0, Carb 11gm, Fib 2gm, Sodium 22mg*

1	cup vinegar
1/2	cup water
1	cup beet juice from can
2	tablespoons sugar or 4 packages artificial sweetener
2	tablespoons pickling spice
1	(16-ounce) can beets, drained, quartered
2	cups thinly sliced onions

Grandma's Potato Salad

Deliciously creamy.

8   medium potatoes, boiled with skin on

3   hard-boiled eggs

1/3 cup diced celery

1/3 cup diced onion

1/3 cup chopped sweet pickles

1   (4-ounce) jar pimiento, chopped

1/2 teaspoon salt

1/4 teaspoon pepper

Dash of paprika

Dressing:

3   tablespoons sugar

1   teaspoon cider vinegar

2   teaspoons yellow mustard

1   cup reduced-fat mayonnaise

Peel and dice the potatoes while warm; put in a large bowl. Peel the eggs and discard the yolks*; dice the whites and add to the potatoes. Add the celery, onion, pickles, pimiento, salt, and pepper; toss gently.

To make the dressing, combine the sugar, vinegar, mustard, and salad dressing in a small bowl; blend well. Pour over the vegetables; toss gently to coat. The dressing coats best if the potatoes are still warm. Sprinkle with paprika. Refrigerate at least 1 hour before serving.

Yield: Approximately 8 (1-cup) servings

* If you prefer to use the egg yolks also, this will change the nutritional values.

Note: I prefer to use red potatoes for this recipe.

1 serving contains: *Cal 238kc, Prot 4gm, Fat 8gm, Chol 10mg, Carb 38gm, Fib 2gm, Sodium 216mg*

Curried Chicken and Pasta Salad

Looks most attractive garnished with melon or pineapple wedges.

Place the chicken in a medium saucepan with the wine, thyme, carrot, onion, water, and $1/4$ teaspoon of the salt. Bring to a boil, reduce the heat and simmer, covered, for about 45 minutes, or until the chicken is tender. Cool the chicken in the broth. Cook the pasta according to package directions; drain. When the chicken is cool, cut into 1-inch cubes and place in a large bowl with the grapes, celery, green onion, and pasta. In a small bowl, blend the yogurt, mayonnaise, honey, lemon juice, curry powder, the remaining $1/2$ teaspoon salt, and pepper. Pour over the chicken mixture and toss. To serve, line a platter or serving bowl with lettuce leaves and spoon chicken salad onto lettuce.

Yield: 8 ($3/4$-cup) servings

1 serving contains: *Cal 168kc, Prot 15gm, Fat 5gm, Chol 40mg, Carb 18gm, Fib 1gm, Sodium 293mg*

4	boneless, skinless whole chicken breasts, about 1 pound
$1/4$	cup white wine
$1/2$	teaspoon dried thyme
1	carrot, quartered
$1/2$	onion, quartered
$3/4$	cup water
$3/4$	teaspoon salt, divided
$1/2$	cup uncooked pasta
2	cups seedless grapes
$1/4$	cup thinly sliced celery
$1/4$	cup thinly sliced green onion
$2 1/2$	tablespoons plain reduced-fat yogurt
$3/4$	cup reduced-fat mayonnaise
$1 1/2$	tablespoons honey
$1 1/2$	teaspoons lemon juice
$1/4$	teaspoon curry powder
Pepper to taste	
Lettuce for garnish	

Mediterranean Salad

1 (8-ounce) package spaghetti, uncooked (or pasta of your choice)

1 (6-ounce) jar marinated artichoke hearts, packed in water drained, coarsely chopped

1 (4-ounce) can of sliced ripe olives, drained

1 large cucumber, cubed

1 medium red bell pepper, chopped

1 small zucchini, chopped

1/2 small purple onion, thinly sliced

1/2 cup reduced-fat mayonnaise

1 teaspoon olive oil

1/2 cup reduced-fat Italian salad dressing

1 teaspoon dried parsley flakes

1/2 teaspoon dried dill weed

1/2 teaspoon freshly ground pepper

1/2 cup freshly grated Parmesan cheese

Cook the spaghetti according to package directions; drain while thoroughly rinsing with cold water. Drain and coarsely chop the artichokes; place in a large mixing bowl with the next 5 ingredients. Add the spaghetti; toss to blend the ingredients. Combine the mayonnaise and remaining ingredients in a separate bowl, stirring with a wire whisk; add to the spaghetti mixture, toss to blend the ingredients. Sprinkle Parmesan cheese over top; cover and chill.

Yield: 8 servings

1 serving contains: *Cal 234kc, Prot 8gm, Fat 9gm, Chol 11mg, Carb 30gm, Fib 3gm, Sodium 512mg*

Pennsylvania Dutch Tomatoes and Onions

A festive, colorful summer dish.

In a medium-size shallow glass dish, alternately layer the tomatoes and onion until all the vegetables are used. Sprinkle the brown sugar over top, then slowly pour the vinegar over the sugar. Cover and refrigerate for 3 to 4 hours until ready to serve. While the salad is in refrigerator, spoon the dressing over the vegetables at least twice. Garnish with parsley sprigs before serving.

Yield: 8 ($^1/_2$-cup) servings

1 serving contains: *Cal 69kc, Prot 1gm, Fat trace, Chol 0, Carb 17gm, Fib 1gm, Sodium 9mg*

3	medium tomatoes, sliced
1	medium sweet onion, thinly sliced
$^1/_2$	cup lightly packed brown sugar
$^1/_4$	cup vinegar, white or flavored
3	parsley sprigs

Clara's Sweet-Tart Vegetable Salad

This colorful dish can take the place of rice, potatoes, or vegetables in your meal.

1 (16-ounce) can French-style green beans, drained

1 (12-ounce) can white corn, drained

1 (17-ounce) can tiny peas, drained

1 cup chopped celery

1/4 cup chopped green onion

1 cup chopped red or green bell pepper

1 (2-ounce) jar pimiento, chopped

Dressing:

3/4 cup vinegar

1/2 cup canola oil

1/2 cup sugar

4 packages artificial sweetener

1 teaspoon celery seed

Pepper to taste

In a large bowl, combine the vegetables. To make dressing, in a small saucepan, combine the vinegar, oil, sugar, sweetener, celery seed, and pepper. Stir the ingredients over medium-low heat just until the sugar is dissolved. Cool, then pour over the vegetables. Cover and refrigerate at least overnight or several days.

Yield: 16 (1/2-cup) servings

1 serving contains: *Cal 135kc, Prot 2gm, Fat 7gm, Chol 0, Carb 17gm, Fib 2gm, Sodium 138mg*

Waldorf Salad

Begin with fresh greens and apples for a successful salad.

In a large bowl, combine the lettuce, apple, and raisins. In a small bowl, blend the yogurt, mayonnaise, cinnamon, and nutmeg. Pour over the salad and toss gently until coated. Serve immediately.

Yield: 9 (^{1}/2-cup) servings

1 serving contains: *Cal 61kc, Prot 1gm, Fat 2gm, Chol 3mg, Carb 12gm, Fib 1gm, Sodium 51mg*

3   cups lettuce,
     torn into bite-size pieces

1   Rome apple, cored,
     cut into bite-size
     pieces

^{1}/2 cup raisins

^{1}/2 cup plain reduced-fat
     yogurt

^{1}/2 cup reduced-fat
     mayonnaise

Dash of ground cinnamon

Dash of ground nutmeg

Wilted Lettuce

A family favorite.

1 head leaf lettuce, rinsed, dried
$1/3$ cup chopped green onion
$1/4$ cup white vinegar
$1/2$ cup water
2 tablespoons canola oil
1 teaspoon sugar

In a large bowl, separate the lettuce leaves and tear into bite-size pieces; add the green onion. In a small saucepan, combine the vinegar, water, oil, and sugar; bring to a boil. Pour over the lettuce and onion; toss gently to coat the lettuce well. Serve immediately.

Yield: 6 (1-cup) servings

1 serving contains: *Cal 48kc, Prot trace, Fat 5gm, Chol 0, Carb 2gm, Fib trace, Sodium 2mg*

Fresh Corn Salad

Yummy crunchy salad.

Cook the corn, covered in boiling water, for 8 to 10 minutes; drain and cool. Combine the corn with the next 5 ingredients. Set aside. Combine the garlic and the next 8 ingredients in a separate bowl. Slowly add the oil, beating constantly with a whisk until well blended and the oil is emulsified. Toss gently with the vegetables. Chill for 8 hours. Serve with slotted spoon.

Yield: 12 servings

✳ Substitute 1 packet artificial sweetener if desired.

1 serving contains: *Cal 92kc, Prot 1gm, Fat 6gm, Chol 0, Carb 9gm, Fib 1gm, Sodium 102mg*

4	ears of corn, about 2 to 3 cups, cut from cob
1/2	cup chopped sweet onion
1/4	cup chopped chives
2	small zucchini, cubed
1	red bell pepper, chopped
1/4	cup chopped parsley
1	garlic clove, minced
1/4	teaspoon salt
3	tablespoons white wine vinegar
1/2	teaspoon hot sauce, optional
	Freshly ground black pepper to taste
1/8	teaspoon cayenne pepper, or to taste
2	teaspoons sugar*
1/2	teaspoon ground cumin
2	teaspoons Dijon mustard
1/3	cup canola oil

Spring Greens with Jicama in Raspberry Vinaigrette

Crunchy jicama, oranges, and walnuts make a great combination.

2   tablespoons sugar

1   teaspoon minced onion

Dash of white Worcestershire sauce

2   tablespoons canola oil

1   tablespoon raspberry vinegar*

1   large orange, peeled and cut into segments

4   cups loosely packed spring greens or spinach**

1/4 jicama, peeled and cut into small cubes***

2   tablespoons walnuts

Place the sugar, onion, and Worcestershire sauce in a blender; with the blender on low, slowly add the oil and raspberry vinegar until thoroughly blended; set aside.

Remove the membrane from orange segments; combine the greens, jicama, and orange segments in a salad bowl. When ready to serve, slowly drizzle the dressing over all, toss gently; then sprinkle with walnuts. Serve immediately.

Yield: 4 servings

*You can substitute rice vinegar or cider vinegar.

**You can substitute any green or red leaf lettuce.

***Jicama is a delightfully crisp tuber, that tastes like a cross between an apple and a potato. It is found in the grocer's produce section.

1 serving contains: *Cal 144kc, Prot 3gm, Fat 10gm, Chol 0, Carb 14gm, Fib 3gm, Sodium 48mg*

Creamy Dressing

Great with leaf lettuce, tomato, and croutons.

In a small bowl, blend all the ingredients. Let stand briefly before serving to blend the flavors.

Yield: 10 (2-tablespoon) servings

1 serving contains: *Cal 38kc, Prot 0, Fat 3gm, Chol 3mg, Carb 5gm, Fib 0, Sodium 133mg*

1 cup reduced-fat mayonnaise
1/4 cup catsup
Dash of red-pepper sauce
1/8 teaspoon vinegar

Sweet-and-Sour Dressing

Perfect for a variety of salads.

In a small bowl, combine all the ingredients. Refrigerate before using.

Yield: 10 (2-tablespoon) servings

1 serving contains: *Cal 47kc, Prot 0, Fat 3gm, Chol 3mg, Carb 7gm, Fib 0, Sodium 83mg*

3 tablespoons sugar
1 teaspoon vinegar
2 teaspoons prepared yellow mustard
1 cup reduced-fat mayonnaise

Tart Horseradish Dressing

Lower in fat and calories than commercial dressing.

½ cup plain reduced-fat yogurt

½ cup reduced-fat mayonnaise

2 tablespoons minced dill pickle

½ teaspoon prepared horseradish

¼ teaspoon prepared brown mustard

¼ cup catsup

Dash of teriyaki sauce

In a small bowl, combine all the ingredients; mix well. Cover and refrigerate for several hours before serving.

Yield: 10 (2-tablespoon) servings

1 serving contains: *Cal 30kc, Prot 1gm, Fat 2gm, Chol 2mg, Carb 4gm, Fib 0, Sodium 203mg*

Vinegar and Oil Dressing

Classic dressing made low-calorie and reduced-fat.

Combine all the ingredients in a cruet; shake well.

Yield: 10 (2-tablespoon) servings

1 serving contains: *Cal 26kc, Prot 0, Fat 1gm, Chol 0, Carb 4gm, Fib 0, Sodium trace*

$3/4$ cup water

$1/4$ cup vinegar

2 tablespoons honey

1 tablespoon extra-virgin olive oil

Poultry

Poultry is one of our favorite foods. It's nutritious because it's high in protein, B vitamins, and minerals. With the exception of duck and goose, it is fairly low in fat and can be made more so by removing skin and any visible fat before cooking.

Chicken is probably the most versatile food in your kitchen. It can be prepared in a wide variety of ways, such as roasting, stove-top casseroles, oven casseroles, or broiling. I believe a clay pot does a wonderful job of "roasting" a chicken, and roast chicken is a remarkably easy dish to prepare.

With all my recipes, you can sauté or stir-fry chicken in a nonstick skillet with a minimal amount of oil. It is not necessary to have the large quantity of oil traditionally used for these dishes.

Turkey is available at the market in many forms year-round. With a little experimentation, you can substitute ground turkey or chicken for ground beef in many of your favorite recipes—it is a welcome change. Turkey breasts have also become quite popular. They are quick and simple to prepare and can provide a great dinner as well as delicious sandwiches for another day.

In this section, you will find a large selection of recipes for varied styles and tastes.

Temperatures for poultry using an instant-read thermometer:

Chicken Breast	**165 degrees**
Turkey Breast	**165 degees**
Turkey Leg	**170 degrees**
Stuffing in bird	**160 degrees**

Poultry Precautions

✦ Wash your hands in hot soapy water before and after handling raw poultry and before handling any other cooking equipment or food.

✦ Always wash the knife, cutting board or any surface that may have had contact with the raw poultry before cutting other foods.

✦ An acrylic cutting board is preferable to a wooden one because it is dishwasher-safe and easier to keep sanitary. Wood surfaces, especially grooves, can harbor bacteria and should be washed twice after use: Once with hot soapy water and a second wash with a solution of 2 teaspoons of chlorine bleach in 1 quart of water. Rinse with clean water.

✦ Always rinse poultry under cold running water before preparing or cooking. Prepare raw meat as soon as it has been rinsed.

✦ Do not let uncooked poultry sit out on the countertop.

✦ Thaw frozen poultry in the refrigerator, microwave, or cold water—not at room temperature on a countertop. If some edges become slightly cooked by the microwave, cook the food immediately and thoroughly to kill any bacterial growth that may have started due to the heat from the microwave.

✦ Refrigerate packaged poultry in store wrapping until used. To freeze, place plastic or foil over store wrapping and freeze. Date and label package and use within 6 months for turkey pieces, 9 months for chicken pieces, and 12 months for whole chicken or turkey.

✦ Refrigerator storage: Fresh poultry 1 to 2 days; cooked poultry covered with broth or gravy 1 to 2 days; cooked poultry dishes 3 to 4 days.

✦ Cold foods should be served cold and hot foods should be served hot. Do not leave cooked poultry out on a buffet or countertop more than two hours because disease-causing bacteria can grow in that time.

✦ Always marinate poultry in the refrigerator rather than at room temperature, even if it's a short time.

✦ Do not serve poultry raw or rare—meat should not be pink and juices should be clear.

✦ Don't buy prestuffed whole birds. Small prestuffed breasts should be safe.

✦ Birds should be stuffed immediately prior to cooking. Loosely pack stuffing into the cavities—do not fill tightly.

Broiled Turkey Cutlets

A quick, flavorful change. Strips of roasted red bell peppers, page 211, make an eye-catching garnish.

Rinse the turkey and pat dry. In a small bowl, combine the oil, lime juice, soy sauce, garlic, onion, cilantro or parsley, and pepper. Pour over the turkey cutlets in a large shallow dish; cover and marinate in the refrigerator for 2 hours. Preheat the oven to broil. Transfer the cutlets from the marinade to a broiler pan, reserving the marinade. Broil the cutlets 4 to 5 inches from the heat source for about 2 minutes on each side or until just tender, basting twice with the reserved marinade; do not overcook. Serve immediately.

Yield: 2 servings

1 serving contains: *Cal 205kc, Prot 28gm, Fat 9gm, Chol 68mg, Carb 4gm, Fib trace, Sodium 587mg*

4	turkey breast cutlets, about 8 ounces
1	tablespoon extra-virgin olive oil
2	tablespoons lime juice
1	tablespoon reduced-sodium soy sauce
1	small garlic clove, minced
2	tablespoons minced onion
1	tablespoon minced cilantro or parsley
Pepper to taste	

Chicken Breasts with Cling Peaches

If fresh peaches are available, use them. Substitute water for the canned peach juice.

4 boneless, skinless chicken breast halves

1/2 cup all-purpose flour

1/2 teaspoon salt

Pepper to taste

4 canned cling peach halves, packed in natural juice, drained, juice reserved

2 tablespoons brown sugar

2 tablespoons Marsala wine

1 teaspoon dried leaf basil

1/4 teaspoon ground allspice

Preheat the oven to 350°F (175°C). Rinse the chicken and pat dry. On a large plate, combine flour, salt, and pepper. Dredge the chicken in the flour mixture; set aside.

Heat a large nonstick skillet over medium-high heat; spray lightly with vegetable spray. Add the chicken and cook quickly until browned on both sides. Place in a medium-size shallow baking dish. Arrange the drained peach halves around the chicken; set baking dish aside.

Add enough water to the reserved peach juice to make 1 cup; pour into a small bowl. Stir in the brown sugar, wine, basil, and allspice. Pour over the chicken and peaches; cover with a lid or foil. Bake for about 45 minutes or until internal temperature is 165°F. To serve, place the chicken and peaches on a serving plate and spoon juices over all.

Yield: 4 servings

1 serving contains: *Cal 252kc, Prot 29gm, Fat 3gm, Chol 73mg, Carb 24gm, Fib 1gm, Sodium 313mg*

Chicken Breast with Apricots and Prunes

A wonderful fruity combination.

Preheat the oven to 350°F (175°C). Rinse the chicken and pat dry. Heat a medium-size nonstick skillet on medium-high heat. Spray for 2 to 3 seconds with vegetable spray; add the chicken and cook until browned on both sides. Put the chicken into a 10-inch shallow baking dish. Add the apricots and prunes, and set aside.

In a small mixing bowl, combine the liqueur, oil, juices, and wine. Pour over the chicken and fruit; cover and bake for 45 to 50 minutes or until the chicken is just tender. Pour the pan drippings into a small saucepan; add the chicken broth. In a small bowl combine the water and cornstarch; stir into the liquid in the pan. Cook over medium-high heat, stirring constantly, until bubbly and thickened. Place the chicken and fruit on serving platter; pour the sauce over the chicken.

Yield: 4 servings

4	boneless, skinless chicken breast halves
1/2	cup dried apricots
1/2	cup dried prunes
1/2	tablespoon apricot liqueur
1/2	tablespoon oil
1/2	cup apple juice
1	teaspooon lemon juice
1/4	cup white wine
1/4	cup reduced-fat, reduced-sodium chicken broth
2	tablespoons cold water
1	tablespoon cornstarch

1 serving contains: *Cal 279kc, Prot 28gm, Fat 5gm, Chol 73mg, Carb 29gm, Fib 3gm, Sodium 115mg*

Fruit-Stuffed Turkey Tenderloins

Serve with broiled tomato halves and bright green sugar snap peas for a company dish.

2　fresh turkey breast tenderloins, about 1 1/4 pounds

1/4　teaspoon salt

Freshly ground pepper to taste

1/3　cup cubed fresh bread

1/2　cup finely diced cooking apple

1/3　cup finely diced prunes

1/4　teaspoon ground allspice

1/4　teaspoon ground nutmeg

2　tablespoons plus 1 teaspoon margarine, melted

Dash of paprika

Preheat the oven to 350°F (175°C). Rinse the turkey and pat dry. Using kitchen shears, cut a pocket lengthwise in the thickest side of each tenderloin. Salt and pepper the inside of the pockets; set aside. In a small bowl, combine the bread, apple, prunes, allspice, and nutmeg. Pour 2 tablespoons margarine over all, tossing well to coat the bread cubes. Spoon the stuffing into the turkey pockets and secure with wooden picks. Place in a medium-size shallow baking dish. Drizzle 1 teaspoon melted margarine over the turkey and dust lightly with paprika. Bake, covered, for 45 to 50 minutes or just until turkey is tender and internal temperature reaches 165°F. Baste occasionally with juices. To serve, cut each tenderloin in half.

Yield: 4 servings

Variation:

✦ Substitute 4 boneless, skinless chicken breast halves for turkey tenderloins. Pound chicken until thin before wrapping each half around 1/4 of the stuffing.

1 serving contains: *Cal 259kc, Prot 34gm, Fat 8gm, Chol 86mg, Carb 13gm, Fib 2gm, Sodium 397mg*

Creamy Chicken Casserole

Substitute turkey for chicken in this flavorful casserole.
Pickled Beets and Onions, page 109, make a lovely accompaniment.

Preheat the oven to 350°F (175°C). In a medium saucepan, combine the flour and powdered milk. Slowly add the skim milk, stirring to blend. Cook over medium heat until the sauce thickens, stirring constantly. Add the salt, pepper, marjoram, and thyme; set aside. In a large nonstick skillet over low heat, cook the celery and mushrooms in 1 tablespoon broth until tender. Stir in rice, 1 cup broth, chicken, and sauce. Pour into a shallow casserole. Sprinkle with parsley. Bake, covered, for 35 minutes; remove the lid and bake for about 10 minutes longer or until bubbling. Serve immediately.

Yield: 6 servings

Variation:

✦ Diet permitting, sprinkle with ¼ cup slivered almonds before baking.

1 serving contains: *Cal 224kc, Prot 19gm, Fat 2gm, Chol 38mg, Carb 31gm, Fib 1gm, Sodium 293mg*

2	tablespoons all-purpose flour
1	tablespoon nonfat powdered milk
1¼	cups skim milk
¼	cup fat-free half-and-half
¼	teaspoon salt
Pepper to taste	
½	teaspoon dried leaf marjoram
½	teaspoon dried leaf thyme
½	cup celery, thinly sliced diagonally
½	cup sliced fresh mushrooms
1	tablespoon plus 1 cup reduced-fat reduced-sodium chicken broth
3	cups cooked rice
2½	cups cubed cooked chicken
1	tablespoon chopped fresh parsley

Soba Noodles with Broccoli and Chicken

The kids love the soba noodles.

6	ounces uncooked soba noodles*
1/4	cup sake or dry sherry or chicken broth
3	tablespoons low-sodium soy sauce
2	tablespoons rice vinegar
1	teaspoon honey
1/4	teaspoon crushed red pepper
1	tablespoon canola oil
1	pound chicken breast tenders, cut into bite-size pieces
1 1/2	teaspoon dark sesame oil
2	cups quartered mushrooms
3	cups broccoli florets
1	cup carrots thinly sliced
1	red bell pepper, cut into 1-inch strips
1	tablespoon grated fresh ginger, or as desired
2	garlic cloves, minced

Cook the noodles according to package directions, drain; set aside. Combine the sherry, soy sauce, vinegar, honey, and red pepper and set aside. Heat canola oil in a large nonstick skillet over medium-high heat. Add the chicken, and stir-fry for 4 minutes or until done. Remove the chicken from the skillet and keep warm. Heat the sesame oil in the same skillet over medium-high heat. Add the mushrooms, broccoli, carrots, bell pepper, ginger, and garlic and stir-fry for 4 minutes or until broccoli is crisp-tender. Return the chicken to the pan, stir in the sherry mixture, and cook for 1 minute or until thoroughly heated. Serve over noodles.

Yield: 4 (1 1/4 cups chicken mixture and 1/2 cup noodles) servings

*With noodles in a colander, run them under hot water to warm them; drain, and serve immediately.

1 serving contains: *Cal 386kc, Prot 37gm, Fat 10gm, Chol 72mg, Carb 42gm, Fib 1gm, Sodium 944mg*

Coq au Vin

My "impress-the-guest" dish served with Rice and Pecan Pilaf, page 222, petite peas and Dinner Rolls, page 82. Although traditionally red wine is used in this classic dish, I prefer the flavor and color of white wine.

Preheat the oven to 350°F (175°C). Rinse the chicken and pat dry. Melt 1 teaspoon butter with 1 teaspoon oil in a large nonstick skillet over medium heat. Add the garlic powder and herbs; stir together 30 seconds. Dredge chicken in flour. Add to the skillet and cook until brown on both sides. Remove to a small casserole; set aside. Add the remaining butter and oil to the skillet. Add the mushrooms and onions; sauté until golden. Add to the casserole. Pour the wine into the skillet and scrape up browned pieces. Pour over the chicken. Bake, covered, for 50 to 60 minutes or until tender. Serve immediately.

Yield: 4 servings

1 serving contains: *Cal 193kc, Prot 28gm, Fat 5gm, Chol 73mg, Carb 5gm, Fib 1gm, Sodium 112mg*

4	boneless, skinless chicken breasts halves
2	teaspoons butter, divided
2	teaspoons extra-virgin olive oil, divided
$1/8$	teaspoon garlic powder
$1/8$	teaspoon dried thyme
$1/8$	teaspoon lemon pepper
$1/2$	teaspoon minced chives
1	tablespoon chopped fresh parsley
1	tablespoon all-purpose flour
4	ounces fresh mushrooms, sliced
4	ounces pearl onions
$1/4$	cup white wine

Angie's Baked Chicken

Deliciously moist, quick and easy. Coleslaw, page 94, is a perfect accompaniment.

4   boneless, skinless chicken breast halves

1   cup fine fresh breadcrumbs

$^3/_4$ teaspoon paprika

$^3/_4$ teaspoon onion powder

$^1/_4$ teaspoon lemon pepper

1   tablespoon canola oil

Preheat the oven to 400°F (205°C). Rinse the chicken and pat dry. Place the breadcrumbs and seasonings in a plastic bag; shake to mix. Add the oil and shake again. Put the chicken in bag 1 piece at a time and shake until well coated. Place in a medium-size shallow baking dish. Bake, uncovered, for 1 hour or until tender. Serve immediately.

Yield: 4 servings

Variation:

✦ Substitute $^1/_4$ cup oat bran for $^1/_4$ cup breadcrumbs.

1 serving contains: *Cal 272kc, Prot 30gm, Fat 8gm, Chol 73mg, Carb 19gm, Fib 0, Sodium 248mg*

Simply Delicious Chicken

Simple to make and delicious to your taste buds.

Preheat the oven to 325°F (170°C). Rinse the chicken and pat dry. Sauté the onions in olive oil in large skillet, cover onions with one teaspoon paprika. Lay the chicken on top of cooked onions; add salt, pepper, and remaining paprika. Cover and cook for approximately 1 hour.

Remove the chicken, then stir in the sour cream. Place the rice on a serving plate, top with the chicken and then the sour cream sauce. Serve over the rice.

Yield: 4 servings

1 serving contains: *Cal 410kc, Prot 38gm, Fat 11gm, Chol 99gm, Carb 39gm, Fib 4gm, Sodium 238mg*

4	boneless, skinless chicken breast halves
1	large onion, chopped
2	teaspoons extra-virgin olive oil
2	teaspoons paprika, divided
1/4	teaspoon salt
1/8	teaspoon freshly ground pepper
1/2	cup reduced-fat sour cream
3	cups cooked brown rice

Lemony Ginger Chicken

Reduced-fat variation of an old favorite.

4	boneless, skinless chicken breast halves
$1/3$	cup lemon juice
1	garlic clove, minced
$1/2$	teaspoon minced fresh ginger root
2	tablespoons all-purpose flour
$1/4$	teaspoon ground ginger
Dash of salt	
Dash of pepper	
2	teaspoons olive oil
1	tablespoon water
1	teaspoon brown sugar
4	thin lemon slices

Rinse the chicken and pat dry. Place in a small, shallow dish. In a small bowl, combine the lemon juice, garlic, and fresh ginger; pour over chicken. Cover and refrigerate at least 1 hour. Preheat the oven to 350°F (175°C). Remove the chicken from the marinade. Combine the flour, ground ginger, salt, and pepper in a plastic bag. Put the chicken in the flour mixture; shake gently to coat. Heat oil in a nonstick skillet over medium heat. Cook the chicken in the oil until brown on both sides. Place the chicken in a small, shallow baking dish. Combine 2 tablespoons reserved marinade and 1 tablespoon water; pour over the chicken. Spoon the brown sugar on top of chicken; place a lemon slice on top of the sugar. Bake, uncovered, for 45 minutes to 1 hour or until tender. Serve immediately.

Yield: 4 servings

1 serving contains: *Cal 234kc, Prot 28gm, Fat 7gm, Chol 73mg, Carb 14gm, Fib trace, Sodium 65mg*

Chicken and Broccoli Casserole

Colorful and delicious.

Preheat the oven to 350°F (175°C). Steam the broccoli until just tender; drain well. Arrange in a shallow baking dish; lay the chicken on top of broccoli. Combine the mayonnaise, lemon juice, curry powder, and white sauce; pour over the chicken. Sprinkle the cheese over all. Combine the breadcrumbs and oat bran, then sprinkle on top of the cheese. Bake, uncovered, for 25 to 30 minutes or until bubbling and brown. Serve immediately.

Yield: 6 servings

1 serving contains: *Cal 265kc, Prot 24gm, Fat 8gm, Chol 49gm, Carb 27gm, Fib 4gm, Sodium 377mg*

6	cups trimmed fresh broccoli or 2 (10-ounce) packages frozen broccoli spears or asparagus
2	cups cooked chicken, cut in bite-size pieces
3/4	cups reduced-fat mayonnaise
1	teaspoon lemon juice
1/2	teaspoon curry powder
1	(10 1/4-ounce) can reduced-fat, reduced-sodium cream of chicken soup or Basic White Sauce with chicken flavoring, page 242
1/2	cup shredded reduced-fat Cheddar cheese
1/2	cup fresh breadcrumbs
2	tablespoons oat bran

135

Chicken and Sweet Potatoes

A ring of sweet potatoes surrounds a chicken filling.

2   cups cooked sweet potatoes, mashed

2   tablespoons brown sugar

$1/2$ teaspoon ground cinnamon

$1/8$ teaspoon ground nutmeg

$1/3$ cup evaporated skim milk

$1/4$ cup chicken broth

$1/4$ cup minced onion

1   (8-ounce) can water chestnuts, drained, sliced

1   ($10^3/4$-ounce) can reduced-fat, reduced-sodium cream of chicken soup or Basic White Sauce with chicken flavoring, page 242

3   cups cubed cooked chicken

3   tablespoons water

Preheat the oven to 350°F (175°C). In a medium-size bowl, combine the sweet potatoes, brown sugar, cinnamon, nutmeg, and milk. Spread around the inside edge of a round 10-inch casserole, forming a ring. In a medium-size nonstick skillet, heat the broth over low heat. Add the onion and water chestnuts; cook until tender. Add the soup or sauce, chicken and water; cook over medium heat until hot, stirring occasionally. Spoon the chicken mixture into the center of the sweet potato ring in the casserole. Bake, uncovered, for 30 minutes or until bubbling.

Yield: 6 (1$1/4$-cup) servings

1 serving contains: *Cal 308kc, Prot 23gm, Fat 6gm, Chol 53mg, Carb 42gm, Fib 2gm, Sodium 510mg*

Chicken and Vegetable Casserole

A great make-ahead one-dish meal.

Preheat the oven to 350°F (175°C). Rinse the chicken and pat dry. Heat a medium-size nonstick skillet over low heat; spray lightly with vegetable spray. Add the chicken and cook until browned on both sides. Transfer the chicken to a medium-size shallow casserole. Add the vegetables to casserole. In a small bowl, combine the broth, soup or sauce, milk, thyme, sage, and bay leaf; pour over chicken and vegetables. Cover and refrigerate until ready to bake. Bake, covered, for 1 hour or until vegetables and chicken are tender. Serve immediately.

Yield: 4 servings

1 serving contains: *Cal 343kc, Prot 32gm, Fat 9gm, Chol 75mg, Carb 32gm, Fib 4gm, Sodium 803mg*

- 4 **boneless, skinless chicken breasts halves**
- 4 **carrots, peeled and quartered**
- 1 **cup pearl onions**
- 2 **celery stalks, cut into large pieces, about 1 $1/2$ cups**
- 2 **potatoes, peeled and quartered, about 2 cups**
- $1/4$ **cup chicken broth**
- 1 **($10^3/4$-ounce) can reduced-fat, reduced-sodium cream of mushroom soup or Basic White Sauce with chicken flavoring, page 242**
- $1/2$ **cup skim milk**
- $1/4$ **teaspoon dried thyme**
- $1/8$ **teaspoon ground sage**
- 1 **bay leaf**

Chicken au Gratin Casserole

Tender chicken in a creamy cheese sauce.

1/4 cup reduced-fat, reduced-sodium chicken broth

1/4 cup all-purpose flour

1 tablespoon nonfat powdered milk

1 1/2 cups skim milk

1/2 cup fat-free half-and-half

1/2 cup shredded reduced-fat sharp Cheddar cheese

3 1/2 cups cubed cooked chicken

Pepper to taste

1/2 cup fresh breadcrumbs

Preheat the oven to 350°F (175°C). Heat the broth in medium-size saucepan over medium heat. In a jar with a lid, combine flour, powdered milk, skim milk, and half-and-half; shake to dissolve. Slowly add milk mixture to broth, stirring constantly until sauce thickens. Add cheese and stir until melted. Gently stir in the chicken; season with pepper. Spoon into a medium-size shallow baking dish. Sprinkle breadcrumbs over all. Bake, uncovered, for 40 minutes or until bubbling. Serve immediately.

Yield: 6 servings

Variations:

✦ Substitute 2 tablespoons oat bran for 2 tablespoons breadcrumbs; add salt to taste.

✦ Slice a few mushrooms and add with the cheese for a flavorful sauce.

1 serving contains: *Cal 206kc, Prot 25gm, Fat 4gm, Chol 57mg, Carb 15gm, Fib trace, Sodium 250mg*

Chicken in Wine Sauce

A simple and delicious one-dish meal.

Preheat the oven to 350°F (175°C). In a large bowl, combine the rice, onion soup mix, mushroom soup or sauce, water, wine, and pimiento. Pour into a large casserole. Rinse the chicken and pat dry. Arrange on top of rice mixture. Sprinkle with paprika and pepper. Bake, covered, for 1 hour or until tender and liquid is absorbed. Serve immediately.

Yield: 4 servings

1 serving contains: *Cal 362kc, Prot 31gm, Fat 9gm, Chol 75m, Carb 34gm, Fib 2gm, Sodium 1133mg*

1	cup uncooked long-grain rice
$1/2$	envelope onion soup mix
1	($10^3/4$-ounce) can reduced-fat, reduced-sodium cream of mushroom soup or Basic White Sauce with mushrooms, page 242
$1^1/2$	cups boiling water
$1/4$	cup white wine
2	tablespoons pimiento
4	boneless, skinless chicken breast halves
$1/4$	teaspoon paprika
Pepper to taste	

Honey Grilled Chicken

Chicken with an intriguing sweet-tart flavor.

4	boneless, skinless chicken breast halves
1/4	cup brown mustard
1/2	cup honey
1	teaspoon curry powder

Rinse the chicken and pat dry. Place the chicken in a medium-size shallow baking dish. In a small saucepan, blend the mustard, honey, and curry powder. Stir until warm over low heat; pour over the chicken, reserving about 1/4 cup divided between 2 separate containers. Cover and marinate in the refrigerator at least 1 hour.

Grease a grill rack; heat grill to medium high. Remove the chicken from marinade. Grill the chicken for about 30 minutes or until tender and the internal temperature reaches 165°F, turning and brushing occasionally with marinade.

Variation:

✦ Place 4 fresh peach halves on the grill for the final 10 minutes of cooking. Cook until tender, basting frequently with the other container of marinade.

Yield: 4 servings

1 serving contains: *Cal 288kc, Prot 28gm, Fat 4gm, Chol 73mg, Carb 35gm, Fib 0, Sodium 270mg*

Grilled Chicken with Herbs

A great low-sodium recipe.

Rinse the chicken and pat dry. Place the chicken in a zip-lock plastic bag. In a small bowl, combine the garlic, oil, rosemary, pepper, sage, and lemon juice. Rinse the chicken and pat dry. Arrange in a medium-size shallow baking dish; pour oil mixture over chicken, reserving $1/8$ cup. Cover and marinate in refrigerator 3 or 4 hours.

Grease grill rack; heat grill to medium high. Remove the chicken from marinade. Place the chicken on a hot grill 3 to 4 inches from coals. Cook 30 to 40 minutes or until internal temperature reaches 165°F, turning and brushing occasionally with reserved marinade. Serve immediately.

Yield: 4 servings

4	boneless, skinless chicken breast halves
1	garlic clove, minced
2	tablespoons canola or olive oil
1	teaspoon dried rosemary
$1/2$	teaspoon pepper
1	teaspoon ground sage
$1/4$	cup lemon juice

1 serving contains: *Cal 209kc, Prot 27gm, Fat 10gm, Chol 73mg, Carb 2gm, Fib trace, Sodium 64mg*

Vineyard Chicken

A perfectly quick and easy recipe for two.

2   boneless, skinless
     chicken breast halves

1/2 cup white wine

1/2 tablespoon lemon juice

1/2 tablespoon extra-virgin
     olive oil

1   green onion, chopped

1   tablespoon minced
     parsley

Dash of pepper

Dash of paprika

Preheat the oven to 350°F (175°C). Spray a small baking pan with vegetable spray; Rinse the chicken and pat dry; place in prepared baking pan. In a small bowl combine the wine, lemon juice, olive oil, green onion, parsley, pepper, and paprika; pour over the chicken. Bake for 50 to 60 minutes or until tender, turning halfway through. Baste occasionally. Serve over rice or pasta.

Yield: 2 servings

1 serving contains: *Cal 266kc, Prot 36gm, Fat 7gm, Chol 96gm, Carb 5gm, Fib 0, Sodium 92mg*

Sweet-and-Sour Grilled Chicken

An interesting combination of flavors.

Preheat a grill to hot. Rinse the chicken and pat dry. Place in a medium-size shallow dish. In a small saucepan, blend the honey, lemon juice, Worcestershire sauce, mustard, wine, basil, and red pepper sauce. Stir until warm over low heat; pour over the chicken. Cover and marinate in refrigerator at least 1 hour. Remove the chicken from marinade, reserving marinade. Place the chicken on a hot grill 3 to 4 inches from coals. Cook 30 to 40 minutes or until tender, turning and brushing occasionally with marinade. Serve immediately.

Yield: 4 servings

1 serving contains: *Cal 269kc, Prot 28gm, Fat 4gm, Chol 73mg, Carb 26gm, Fib trace, Sodium 294mg*

- 4   boneless, skinless chicken breast halves
- $1/3$ cup honey
- $1/3$ cup lemon juice
- 2   tablespoons Worcestershire sauce
- 3   tablespoons brown mustard
- $1/2$ cup white wine
- $1/4$ tablespoon crushed dried basil
- $1/4$ teaspoon red pepper sauce

Chicken Tetrazzini

Terrific with a green salad.

1	cup sliced fresh mushrooms
1/2	cup chopped onion
1 2/3	cups reduced-fat, reduced-sodium chicken broth
2	tablespoons all-purpose flour
1	cup evaporated skim milk
1/4	cup white wine
1/2	teaspoon salt
Pepper to taste	
1/2	cup grated Parmesan cheese
6	ounces spaghetti
1 1/2	cups diced cooked chicken

Preheat the oven to 350°F (175°C). In a large nonstick skillet over low heat, cook the mushrooms and onion in 2 tablespoons chicken broth until tender. Remove from the skillet; set aside. In a jar with a lid, combine flour, remaining chicken broth, and evaporated milk; shake until completely dissolved. Add to the skillet and cook over medium heat, stirring constantly until thickened. Remove from the heat and stir in wine, salt, pepper, and 1/4 cup Parmesan cheese; set aside. While preparing the sauce, cook spaghetti according to package directions; drain well. Combine the spaghetti, mushrooms, onion, and chicken in a medium-size shallow baking dish. Pour sauce over all and sprinkle with remaining cheese. Bake, uncovered, for 25 minutes or until bubbling. Serve immediately.

Yield: 4 servings

1 serving contains: *Cal 411kc, Prot 37gm, Fat 7gm, Chol 68mg, Carb 38gm, Fib 1gm, Sodium 727mg*

Pasta with Chicken

Chicken cubes are a delightful surprise.

Rinse the chicken, pat dry and cut into small cubes, set aside. In a large nonstick skillet over low heat, cook the onion and green pepper in water until tender. Add the mushrooms and stir briskly about 2 minutes. Stir in the spaghetti sauce and simmer at least 30 minutes. While the sauce is cooking, dredge chicken in flour, salt, and pepper. In another large nonstick skillet over medium-high heat, heat $^1/_2$ teaspoon oil and garlic about 5 seconds, stirring briskly; transfer garlic to sauce. Add the remaining oil to skillet; add the chicken and stir-fry over medium-high heat until chicken is tender. In a large kettle, cook the pasta according to package directions. Ten minutes before serving, add the chicken to the sauce and simmer just until heated through. Arrange the pasta on a large platter and spoon sauce with chicken over all. Serve immediately.

Yield: 6 servings

1 serving contains: *Cal 299kc, Prot 20gm, Fat 8gm, Chol 37mg, Carb 39gm, Fib 1gm, Sodium 527mg*

3	boneless, skinless chicken breast halves
$^1/_2$	cup chopped onion
$^1/_2$	cup chopped green bell pepper
$^1/_4$	cup water
$^1/_2$	cup sliced fresh mushrooms
2	cups Marinara Sauce, page 243, or spaghetti sauce of choice
1	tablespoon all-purpose flour
$^1/_4$	teaspoon salt
	Freshly ground black pepper to taste
2	teaspoons olive oil
1	garlic clove, minced
8	ounces spaghetti or pasta of choice

Grilled Jalapeño Chicken

Jalapeños add a nice kick to the grilled chicken.

4	boneless, skinless chicken breast halves
1/2	cup lime juice
1/2	cup honey
2	tablespoons chopped fresh parsley or cilantro
1	jalapeño, diced
2	teaspoons reduced-sodium soy sauce
4	cloves garlic, chopped

Rinse the chicken and pat dry; place in a zip-lock plastic bag. Place lime juice, honey, parsley, jalapeño, soy sauce, and garlic in a blender, process, and pour marinade over the chicken, reserving 1/4 cup of marinade. Close securely and marinate overnight, or for several hours.

Grease grill rack and heat grill to medium high. Grill the chicken for about 30 minutes or until tender and the internal temperature reaches 165°F, turning and brushing with reserved marinade frequently.

Yield: 4 servings

1 serving contains: *Cal 331kc, Prot 36gm, Fat 4gm, Chol 96mg, Carb 40 gm, Fib 0, Sodium 184mg*

Chicken-Stuffed Pasta Shells

A good dish for company; make it early in the day.

Lightly spray a 13 x 9-inch baking dish with vegetable spray. In a large bowl, combine the chicken, parsley, egg white, cottage cheese, pimiento, salt, and pepper; mix well. Using a teaspoon, stuff shells with the mixture. Place the stuffed shells in prepared baking dish. Preheat the oven to 350°F (175°C). In a saucepan, cook the green onion in 2 tablespoons broth until tender. In a jar with a lid, combine the flour, cornstarch and ½ cup broth; shake until dissolved. Add to the onion in saucepan. Cook, stirring constantly, until the mixture starts to boil and thicken; cook 1 minute longer. Gradually add the remaining broth, milk, wine, and cheese, stirring until cheese is melted. Remove from the heat and add salt and pepper. Spoon the sauce over shells; sprinkle with Parmesan cheese. Bake, uncovered, for 30 minutes or until bubbling. Serve immediately.

Yield: 10 (1-shell) servings

1 serving contains: *Cal 172kc, Prot 18gm, Fat 4gm, Chol 32mg, Carb 14gm, Fib trace, Sodium 485mg*

10 to 12 large pasta shells, cooked

Filling:

1½ cups finely shredded cooked chicken

2 tablespoons minced fresh parsley

1 egg white, slightly beaten

1 cup reduced-fat cottage cheese

2 tablespoons finely chopped pimiento

Salt and pepper to taste

Sauce:

¼ cup chopped green onion

1⅓ cups reduced-fat, reduced-sodium chicken broth

2 tablespoons all-purpose flour

1 tablespoon cornstarch

¼ cup evaporated skim milk or fat-free half-and-half

¼ cup white wine

½ cup shredded reduced-fat Cheddar cheese

½ teaspoon salt

Black pepper to taste

2 tablespoons grated Parmesan cheese

147

Chicken Chili

Our favorite chili. Corn Bread, page 73, rounds it out perfectly.
I keep a batch in my freezer.

2	boneless, skinless chicken breast halves
1/2	cup coarsely chopped green bell pepper
1/2	cup coarsely chopped onion
3/4	cup water, divided
3	tablespoons chili seasoning mix
8	ounces tomato sauce
1/4	cup chopped canned green chilies
1 1/2	cups cooked kidney beans
1 1/2	cups cooked pinto beans

Chop the chicken into very small pieces; set aside. In a large nonstick skillet over low heat, cook the green pepper and onion in 2 tablespoons water until tender; remove from skillet and set aside. Add the chicken and 2 tablespoons water to skillet; cook until tender. Add the seasoning mix and stir well. Stir in the tomato sauce, green chilies, beans, 1/2 cup water, and green pepper mixture. Simmer about 30 minutes, stirring occasionally. Serve immediately.

Yield: 6 servings

1 serving contains: *Cal 222kc, Prot 19gm, Fat 2gm, Chol 24mg, Carb 33gm, Fib 6gm, Sodium 300mg*

Southwest Chicken Enchiladas

Serve with Margaritas and baked corn chips.
Shredded lettuce and Refried Beans, page 208, are natural accompaniments.

Preheat the oven to 350°F (175°C). In a medium-size bowl, combine the chicken, tomatoes, chilies, chili powder, onion, and ½ cup cheese. Add about ¾ cup salsa; mix well. Pour remaining salsa in a shallow, wide dish. Dip a tortilla in salsa and lay on a plate. Place about ⅓ cup chicken mixture in a strip toward one side of tortilla; roll up and place in a 13 x 9-inch casserole. Repeat with remaining tortillas and chicken mixture. Pour remaining salsa over filled enchiladas; sprinkle remaining cheese over all. Bake, covered, for 30 minutes. Serve immediately.

Yield: 5 (2-enchilada) servings

1 serving contains: *Cal 416kc, Prot 31gm, Fat 14gm, Chol 60mg, Carb 51gm, Fib 1gm, Sodium 920mg*

2	cups shredded, cooked chicken
½	cup chopped tomatoes, small but not fine
¼	cup chopped canned green chilies
¼	teaspoon ground chili powder
⅓	cup chopped onion
1	cup (4 ounces) shredded reduced-fat Cheddar cheese, divided
4	cups salsa
10	small flour tortillas

Chicken Fajitas

A fun meal, great for a casual dinner. Serve Refried Beans, page 208, on the side.

4	boneless, skinless chicken breast halves
1	cup oil-free Italian salad dressing
1¹/₂	cups salsa
1	teaspoon canola oil
1	garlic clove, minced
1	cup coarsely chopped onion
1	cup coarsely chopped green bell pepper

Dash of ground cumin

Pepper to taste

1	medium-size tomato, cut into small wedges
¹/₂	cup reduced-fat sour cream
8	flour tortillas, warmed
¹/₂	cup shredded reduced-fat Cheddar cheese or Mexican blend cheese
1¹/₂	cups salsa

Rinse the chicken and pat dry. Place in a zip-lock plastic bag. Pour the salad dressing over the chicken; zip the bag closed and refrigerate several hours or overnight.

Grease a grill rack. Heat grill to medium high. Grill the chicken for 30 to 40 minutes or until tender and internal temperature reaches 165°F. Remove from the grill; set aside. In a large nonstick skillet, heat oil over medium heat. Add garlic, onion, and green pepper; sauté until tender. Stir in cumin and pepper. Slice chicken into finger-size pieces. When vegetables are tender, add chicken pieces and toss together; spoon into a serving dish.

To serve, take 1 tortilla and spoon 3 tablespoons chicken mixture into center of tortilla, leaving the bottom free. Add tomato wedges, about 1 tablespoon of sour cream, 1 tablespoon Cheddar cheese, and salsa to taste. Fold bottom of tortilla up, then fold each side in toward center, making a filled pocket.

Yield: 4 (2-fajita) servings

1 serving contains: *Cal 461kc, Prot 42gm, Fat 16gm, Chol 95mg, Carb 57gm, Fib 1gm, Sodium 1031mg*

Serving suggestions: You can add shredded lettuce, avocado, and more salsa to the fajitas.

Ground Turkey Taco Filling

For a Mexican treat, serve with Spanish Lima Beans, page 202, or steamed rice.

In a large nonstick skillet over medium-low heat, cook the ground turkey until almost done; add the onion and cook until tender. Quickly stir in the flour, blending well. Stir in cumin and salt, then the tomato sauce. Simmer over low heat at least 10 minutes. Fill the taco or tostada shells and garnish as desired.

Yield: 6 (2-taco) servings

1 serving contains: *Cal 253kc, Prot 25gm, Fat 8gm, Chol 58mg, Carb 20gm, Fib trace, Sodium 684mg*

1　pound ground turkey

1/3　cup chopped onion

2　tablespoons all-purpose flour

1/2　teaspoon ground cumin

Salt to taste

1　(8-ounce) can tomato sauce

12　taco or tostada shells (made with acceptable oil)

Toppings:

Shredded lettuce

Shredded reduced-fat cheese

Salsa

Chopped green onion

Sliced radishes

Audrey's Oriental Chicken

Serve this when you want something delicious and different for company dinner. Serve with plain boiled rice.

4	boneless, skinless chicken breast halves
1/4	cup firmly packed brown sugar
2	tablespoons cornstarch
1/4	cup vinegar
1	tablespoon reduced-sodium soy sauce
1	(15-ounce) can pineapple chunks, packed in natural juice
1	cup green bell pepper strips
1	cup thin onion rings
1	tablespoon canola oil

Rinse the chicken, pat dry, and cut into strips; set aside. In a medium-size bowl, combine sugar and cornstarch. Gradually stir in the vinegar and soy sauce. Stir in the pineapple, green pepper, and onion; set aside. Heat the oil in a wok or large non-stick skillet over medium-high heat. Add the chicken and stir-fry quickly, just until tender and chicken has turned white. Remove from the skillet and keep warm. Add the pineapple and vegetable mixture; stir until well mixed. Reduce the heat, cover, and simmer over low heat for 15 minutes. When the vegetables are crisp-tender, add the chicken and heat through. Serve immediately.

Yield: 4 (1 1/4-cup) servings

1 serving contains: *Cal 314kc, Prot 28gm, Fat 7gm, Chol 73mg, Carb 36gm, Fib 2gm, Sodium 202mg*

Johnny's Pot Pie

Our son's hearty wintertime favorite.

In a large saucepan, cook the carrots, onion, celery, lima beans, and thyme in boiling water for 10 minutes. Add the potatoes and cook until tender. Add the peas and cook until tender. In a jar with a lid combine the flour, 1 cup milk, and powdered milk; shake until completely dissolved. Pour into a separate saucepan, stirring constantly over medium heat. Add the salt and pepper; stir constantly until thickened. Stir in the remaining 1/2 cup milk and chicken. Stir the vegetables into the chicken mixture; mix well. Pour into a 9-inch square baking dish. Preheat the oven to 450°F (230°C). In a bowl, combine the Baking Mix and margarine; add hot water and stir until dough forms a soft ball. With floured hands, flatten dough into a 9-inch square. Gently roll up the dough and place on top of the chicken mixture. Unroll to fit dish. Bake for about 8 minutes or until browned. Let the pie stand for a few minutes before serving.

Yield: 6 servings

Note: This could easily be made with frozen vegetables instead of fresh vegetables.

1 serving contains: *Cal 357kc, Prot 28gm, Fat 7gm, Chol 50mg, Carb 45gm, Fib 5gm, Sodium 505mg*

2	carrots, chopped
1	onion, chopped
1/2	cup chopped celery
1	cup baby lima beans
1/2	teaspoon dried thyme
2	small potatoes, chopped
1	cup frozen peas
1/4	cup all-purpose flour
1 1/2	cups skim milk, divided
2	tablespoons nonfat powdered milk
1/2	teaspoon salt or less
1/4	teaspoon pepper
2 to 3	cups chopped cooked chicken
1 1/4	cups Baking Mix, page 66 or reduced-fat Bisquick
2	tablespoons margarine, room temperature
5	tablespoons very hot water

Chicken Dinner in a Pot

A perfect Sunday meal to cook in the oven while at church.

Serve Homemade Biscuits, page 67, on the side for a Southern touch.

1	(5- to 6-pound) roasting chicken

Salt to taste, optional

$1/2$ cup white wine

$1/4$ teaspoon dried rosemary

1 small bay leaf

$1/2$ cup chopped celery

1 medium onion, cut into wedges

6 carrots, peeled and cut into chunks

6 potatoes, peeled and quartered

Preheat the oven to 350°F (175°C). Rinse the chicken inside and out; pat dry. Rub the inside of the chicken with salt, if desired; place in a roasting pan. Add the wine, rosemary, and bay leaf. Bake, covered, for about 45 minutes. Add the celery, onion, and carrots; cook for about 30 minutes longer. Add the potatoes and cook for 1 hour longer or until everything is tender. Serve immediately.

Yield: 6 servings

1 serving contains: *Cal 306kc, Prot 28gm, Fat 5gm, Chol 73mg, Carb 33gm, Fib 3gm, Sodium 95mg*

Curried Chicken

Curry enhances the flavor of baked chicken. Accompany with fresh fruit and a plain rice dish.

Preheat the oven to 350°F (175°C). Rinse the chicken and pat dry; dredge in flour. Spray a large nonstick skillet with vegetable spray; heat over medium heat. Add the chicken and cook just until brown; turn and brown the other side. Put the chicken in a medium-size shallow casserole. In a skillet over low heat, cook the onion in the water for 5 minutes; add the apple and cook for 1 minute. Spoon over the chicken; sprinkle with the spices. Pour the broth over all. Bake, uncovered, for 55 minutes or until tender. Add the raisins and cook for 5 minutes longer. Serve immediately.

Yield: 6 servings

1 serving contains: *Cal 214kc, Prot 29gm, Fat 4gm, Chol 73mg, Carb 16gm, Fib 2gm, Sodium 357mg*

6	boneless, skinless chicken breast halves
3	tablespoons all-purpose flour
1½	cups sliced onion
1	tablespoon water
1	apple, peeled, chopped
¼	teaspoon curry powder
⅛	teaspoon ground ginger
⅛	teaspoon ground turmeric
½	teaspoon salt
⅛	teaspoon pepper
1	cup reduced-fat, reduced-sodium chicken broth
⅓	cup raisins

Turkey Loaf

Serve hot with potatoes and Coleslaw, page 94. Slice the cold leftovers for delicious sandwiches.

About ³/4 cup coarsely crushed Wheaties or Cornflakes

¹/4 cup oat bran or ¹/4 cup cereal crumbs

³/4 cup skim milk

2 egg whites

¹/4 cup chopped onion

¹/4 cup chopped green bell pepper

¹/2 teaspoon ground sage

¹/2 teaspoon salt

¹/8 teaspoon pepper

1 teaspoon parsley flakes

1 pound ground turkey

2 tablespoons brown sugar

¹/4 cup catsup

1 teaspoon dry mustard

¹/4 teaspoon ground nutmeg

¹/8 teaspoon ground ginger

Preheat the oven to 350°F (175°C). In a large bowl, combine the crushed cereal, oat bran, milk, egg whites, onion, green pepper, sage, salt, pepper, and parsley; mix well. Add the ground turkey and blend thoroughly. The turkey mixture should be firm enough to shape: if not, add more cereal crumbs. Spoon the mixture into a shallow 2-quart casserole and form into a dome shape or press into a 9 x 5-inch loaf pan; set aside. In a small bowl, combine the brown sugar, catsup, mustard, nutmeg, and ginger; pour over the turkey loaf. Bake, uncovered, for 1 hour. Serve immediately.

Yield: 6 servings

1 serving contains: *Cal 166kc, Prot 20gm, Fat 3gm, Chol 49mg, Carb 15gm, Fib 1, Sodium 390mg*

Stir-Fried Chicken and Vegetables

A quick, easy dish if you prepare the vegetables ahead. Serve with plain boiled rice.

Rinse the chicken, pat dry, and cut into thin strips; heat 1 teaspoon oil in a wok or nonstick skillet over medium heat; add the chicken and stir-fry until the chicken becomes white and is tender, remove from the wok or skillet, keep warm; set aside.

In a small bowl, combine the cornstarch and broth. Stir in the soy sauce and corn syrup; set aside. In a large wok or nonstick skillet, heat 1 tablespoon oil over medium-high heat; add the garlic and ginger root, stirring about 5 seconds, then add the vegetables. Stir-fry quickly for about 1 minute to coat with oil, then reduce heat and cook about 3 minutes longer. Return the chicken to skillet. Stir the cornstarch mixture and add to the skillet, stirring constantly. Bring to a gentle boil. Cook for 30 seconds or until sauce thickens. Serve immediately.

Yield: 4 servings

1 serving contains: *Cal 261kc, Prot 22gm, Fat 8gm, Chol 55mg, Carb 25gm, Fib 2gm, Sodium 173mg*

3	boneless, skinless chicken breast halves
2	tablespoons cornstarch
1/2	cup chicken broth
2	tablespoons reduced-sodium soy sauce
1/4	cup light corn syrup
1	tablespoon plus 1 teaspoon canola oil
1	garlic clove, minced
1	thin slice fresh ginger root
4	cups vegetables, cut for stir-frying

Serving suggestions:

✦ Green, red, or yellow bell peppers (cut into medium slices), broccoli flowerets, carrots (thinly sliced), cauliflower (thinly sliced), mushrooms (thickly sliced), onions (thinly sliced), whole snow peas, water chestnuts (medium sliced)

Stuffed Peppers

A great meal to make ahead and freeze.

4   medium-size green bell peppers, tops and seeds removed, washed

$1/2$ cup chopped onion

2   tablespoons water

8   ounces ground turkey

$3/4$ cup cooked brown rice

$1/4$ teaspoon salt

$1/8$ teaspoon black pepper

$1/8$ teaspoon garlic powder

1   teaspoon Worcestershire sauce

1   ($10^1/2$-ounce) can reduced-fat, reduced-sodium tomato soup, divided

Preheat the oven to 350°F (175°C). Bring a large saucepan filled with water to a boil; add the green peppers and return to a boil. Reduce the heat to medium and cook for 5 minutes. Remove the peppers from the water and drain upside down on a paper towel. In a large nonstick skillet over medium-low heat, cook the onion in 2 tablespoons water. Add the ground turkey and cook, stirring occasionally, until the turkey loses its pink color. Add the rice, salt, black pepper, garlic powder, Worcestershire sauce, and $1/2$ can tomato soup. Stir until well blended. Using a large spoon, fill the green peppers with the turkey mixture. Set upright in a 9 x 5-inch loaf pan. Spoon the remaining soup over top of the peppers. Bake, uncovered, for 30 minutes. Serve immediately.

Yield: 4 servings

1 serving contains: *Cal 163kc, Prot 11gm, Fat 3gm, Chol 23mg, Carb 25gm, Fib 2gm, Sodium 694mg*

Chicken Smothered in Sour Cream

Yummy served over noodles.

Preheat the oven to 350°F (175°C); spray a 2-quart casserole with vegetable spray.

Rinse the chicken, pat dry, and set aside.

Heat the oil in a medium nonstick skillet over medium-high heat; add the onions and sauté for about 5 minutes or until tender. Spoon into the prepared casserole and sprinkle with half the paprika. Place the chicken over the onions and sprinkle with the salt, pepper, and remaining paprika. Bake, covered, for about 50 minutes or until chicken is tender. Remove the chicken, stir in the sour cream, blending well; return the chicken to the sour cream mixture when ready to serve.

Yield: 4 servings

4	boneless, skinless chicken breast halves
2	teaspoons extra-virgin olive oil
1	large onion
1/2	teaspoon salt
1/8	teaspoon freshly ground black pepper
1 1/2	teaspoons paprika, divided
1/2	cup reduced-fat sour cream

Serving suggestion:

✦ Serve over noodles or rice with Green Beans with Walnuts, page 200.

1 serving contains: *Cal 263kc, Prot 37gm, Fat 10gm, Chol 108gm, Carb 5gm, Fib 1gm, Sodium 389mg*

Cooked Chicken

The basis for a wide variety of dishes.

4	boneless, skinless chicken breasts halves
1	bay leaf
1	teaspoon dried thyme
1/2	teaspoon salt
1/2	onion, quartered
1/2	cup white wine, optional

Rinse the chicken. Place the chicken, bay leaf, thyme, salt, onion, and wine, if using, in a large pot; add enough water to cover chicken. Simmer for 45 to 50 minutes or until chicken is tender, being careful not to overcook. Cool the chicken in broth. Discard the onion and bay leaf. The broth can be used immediately or frozen for later use. The chicken can be chopped and used in casseroles, salads, soups, or many other dishes.

Yield: 4 servings

1 serving contains: *Cal 151kc, Prot 27gm, Fat 3gm, Chol 73mg, Carb 2gm, Fib trace, Sodium 308mg*

Seafood

If fresh and prepared properly, fish is a delicious entree. It is lower in calories, saturated fat and in most cases (except in shrimp and lobster), lower in cholesterol than beef, pork, or lamb. Fish is an excellent source of protein, B vitamins and many minerals. Cold-water fish—such as salmon—is a good source of the omega-3 fatty acids, which have been shown to lower lipid levels. Aside from all the health benefits, fish is about the quickest entree to cook and it can be prepared in many ways.

I grew up near a freshwater lake with an avid fisherman father. We ate lots of fish, but it was always fried. I grew up thinking baked fish was for sick people. There are many people who still have this misconception. I hope my recipes will change your opinion of fish.

I highly recommend Linguine and Clam Sauce, page 172. It is one of the easiest recipes in this book, yet good enough to serve your guests. Try one of the scallop recipes—scallops are one of my favorite seafood dishes. Sautéed Scallops, page 179, is simple and delicious. Brenda's Breaded Fish, page 168, is a family favorite dish. Using good quality fish, this combination results in an excellent entrée. For a different taste, try Lemon-Soy Fish Fillets, page 171. Be sure to let the fish marinate to develop the full oriental flavor. Serve with rice and steamed vegetable for a delicious, nutritious, and easily prepared meal.

Frozen fish is an excellent alternative to fresh fish if it is thawed slowly in the refrigerator. As with most foods, never refreeze once it has thawed.

Fish can be prepared in a variety of ways and the basic techniques are explained in the box on page 164. Be careful not to overcook fish; cook until a instant-read thermometer reads 137°F. Serve as soon as it is ready.

General Guidelines
For Cooking Fish

To Broil Fish: Preheat broiler with oven door ajar. Lightly oil rack, unless oil is used on fish. Broil fillets 3 to 4 inches from heat source 4 to 5 minutes or until fish flakes easily. Cook thicker pieces 10 minutes per inch. Only thick pieces need to be turned.

To Grill Fish: Preheat grill. Lightly rub grill rack with oil. Grill fillets 6 to 8 minutes or until fish flakes easily. Cook directly on grill rack, in a fish-grilling basket or in foil boats.

To Poach Fish: Put poaching liquid or a combination of water, herbs, and wine in a large shallow pan or skillet. Add fish and bring to a boil. Reduce heat and simmer until fish flakes easily, about 10 minutes for a 1-inch-thick piece of fish.

To Steam Fish in Foil: Lay fish in center of a large piece of heavy-duty aluminum foil. Add remaining ingredients. Fold foil over fish and seal edges tightly. Bake in preheated oven or on a grill until fish flakes easily.

So-Easy Fish

Delightful recipe for a busy day.

P reheat the oven to 425°F (220°C). Rinse fish and pat dry. Lightly grease a small shallow baking pan with some of the oil. Rub the remaining oil over the top of the fish. In a small bowl, combine the remaining ingredients and sprinkle over the fish. Bake, uncovered, for about 20 minutes or until fish flakes easily. Serve immediately.

Yield: 2 servings

2	fillets white fish, about 8 ounces
$1/2$	teaspoon canola oil
$1/4$	cup fresh breadcrumbs
1	teaspoon grated Parmesan cheese
$1/8$	teaspoon garlic powder
$1/8$	teaspoon lemon pepper

Variation:

✦ Substitute 1 tablespoon oat bran for 1 tablespoon bread-crumbs.

1 serving contains: *Cal 169kc, Prot 24gm, Fat 3gm, Chol 56mg, Carb 9gm, Fib 0, Sodium 204mg*

Baked Fish and Herbs

Serve with Brown Rice Pilaf, page 205, and a colorful vegetable.

4   fillets white fish,
    about 1 pound

2   green onions,
    thinly sliced

1   tablespoon chopped fresh
    parsley

1/4 teaspoon dried mixed
    Italian herbs

1/8 teaspoon lemon pepper

1   firm tomato, sliced

1/8 cup white wine

1   tablespoon lemon juice

1   tablespoon margarine
    or butter, melted

Cherry tomatoes

Preheat the oven to 400°F (205°C). Lightly spray a medium-size shallow baking pan with vegetable spray. Rinse the fish and pat dry. Arrange the fish in a baking pan. Sprinkle the green onions over fish. In a small bowl, mix together the parsley, Italian herbs, and lemon pepper. Sprinkle half of the mixture over the fish and onions. Lay the tomato slices over fish and sprinkle with remaining herbs. In a small bowl, combine the wine and lemon juice. Pour over the fish, then drizzle margarine over all. Bake, uncovered, for 15 to 20 minutes or until fish flakes easily. Garnish with cherry tomatoes. Serve immediately.

Yield: 4 servings

1 serving contains: *Cal 133kc, Prot 22gm, Fat 3gm, Chol 55mg, Carb 4gm, Fib 1gm, Sodium 131mg*

Baked Fish with Tomatoes

An easy, low-calorie entrée.

Preheat the oven to 400°F (205°C). Lightly spray a small shallow baking pan with vegetable spray. Rinse the fish and pat dry. Arrange the fish in the baking pan and place tomato halves around the fish. Sprinkle the lemon peel, pepper, and herbs over fish and tomatoes; drizzle melted margarine over all. Bake, uncovered, for 20 minutes or until fish flakes easily. Serve immediately.

Yield: 2 servings

1 serving contains: *Cal 157kc, Prot 23gm, Fat 4gm, Chol 55mg, Carb 6gm, Fib 2gm, Sodium 173mg*

2   fillets white fish, about 8 ounces

2   firm tomatoes, cut in half

$1/8$ teaspoon grated lemon peel

Pepper to taste

$1/2$ teaspoon oregano

$1/2$ tablespoon snipped chives

$1/4$ teaspoon dill weed

1   tablespoon margarine or butter, melted

Brenda's Breaded Fish

Grandson Joseph loves fish prepared this way.

4   fillets white fish,
    about 1 pound

2   cups loosely packed fresh
    breadcrumbs*

1/3 cup grated Parmesan
    cheese

1   egg white

1   tablespoon water

1/8 teaspoon lemon pepper

Dash of garlic powder

1   tablespoon margarine or
    butter**, melted

Parsley sprigs for garnish

Lemon wedges for garnish

Preheat the oven to 375°F (190°C). Rinse the fish and pat dry. In a small bowl, mix the breadcrumbs and Parmesan cheese. In another small bowl, beat the egg white with the water. Dip the fish in the egg white, then dredge in the breadcrumbs to coat well. Lightly spray a medium-size shallow baking pan with vegetable spray. Arrange the fish in the baking pan and sprinkle with the lemon pepper and garlic powder. Drizzle the margarine over the fish. Bake, uncovered, for about 20 minutes or until the fish flakes easily. If the top doesn't brown nicely, put under the broiler for a few seconds. Garnish with parsley sprigs and lemon wedges. Serve immediately.

Yield: 3 servings

* Substitute 1/2 cup oat bran for 1/2 cup breadcrumbs.

** For less fat, omit the melted margarine and spray breaded fish with vegetable spray before baking.

1 serving contains: *Cal 256kc, Prot 30gm, Fat 8gm, Chol 63mg, Carb 15gm, Fib 1gm, Sodium 514mg*

Crispy Baked Fish and Herbs

You'll like crispy baked fish.

Preheat the oven to 400°F (205°C). Lightly spray a medium-size shallow baking pan with vegetable spray. Rinse the fish and pat dry. In a small bowl, beat the egg white with water. Dip the fish in the egg white, then roll in the cornflake crumbs. Arrange the fish in baking pan. Sprinkle with the lemon pepper and parsley, then drizzle the margarine over all. Bake, uncovered, for about 20 minutes or until the fish flakes easily. Serve immediately.

Yield: 4 servings

4	fillets white fish, about 1 pound
1	egg white
1	tablespoon water
$1/2$	cup cornflake crumbs*
$1/8$	teaspoon lemon pepper
2	teaspoons chopped fresh parsley
1	teaspoon margarine**, melted

* Substitute 2 tablespoons oat bran for 2 tablespoons cereal crumbs.

** For less fat, omit the melted margarine and spray breaded fish with vegetable spray before baking.

1 serving contains: *Cal 135kc, Prot 23gm, Fat 2gm, Chol 55mg, Carb 5gm, Fib trace, Sodium 187mg*

Fish Rolls

For a lovely meal, serve with Cabbage Salad, page 100, Gingered Carrots, page 210, and Brown Rice Pilaf, page 205.

4	fillets white fish, about 1 pound
3	tablespoons finely chopped celery
3	tablespoons finely chopped green onion
2	teaspoons chopped fresh parsley
1	tablespoon chopped pimiento
1/3	cup chicken broth, reduced-fat, reduced-sodium divided
1/2	cup plus 1 tablespoon fresh breadcrumbs
1	tablespoon margerine or butter, melted
1/8	teaspoon grated lemon peel

Pepper to taste

Lime wedges for garnish

Preheat the oven to 375°F (190°C). Lightly spray a shallow baking pan with vegetable spray. Rinse the fish and pat dry; lay fish on a clean work surface. In a medium-size nonstick skillet over low heat, cook the celery, onion, parsley, and pimiento in 1 tablespoon chicken broth until tender. Add the remaining broth and enough breadcrumbs to make a firm mixture. Divide bread mixture evenly over fish fillets; roll up each fillet and secure with a wooden pick. Arrange the fish in the baking pan. Drizzle margarine over all, then sprinkle with lemon peel and pepper. Bake, uncovered, for about 20 minutes or until the fish flakes easily. Garnish with lime wedges. Serve immediately.

Yield: 4 servings

1 serving contains: *Cal 144kc. Prot 23gm, Fat 3gm, Chol 55mg, Carb 6gm, Fib 1gm, Sodium 229mg*

Lemon-Soy Fish Fillets

Soy sauce and ginger give an Oriental flavor.

Rinse the fish and pat dry; lay it in a shallow dish. In a small bowl, combine the margarine, soy sauce, lemon juice, Worcestershire sauce, ginger, garlic, lemon peel, black pepper, and sugar. Pour over the fish and marinate for 2 hours in the refrigerator.

Preheat the broiler. Remove the fish from marinade, reserving marinade. Place the fish in a broiling pan. Broil the fish for 4 to 5 minutes or until it flakes easily, basting with the marinade at least twice. Garnish the fish with parsley and lemon wedges. Serve immediately.

Yield: 2 servings

1 serving contains: *Cal 139kc, Prot 23gm, Fat 2gm, Chol 55mg, Carb 7gm, Fib trace, Sodium 644mg*

2	fillets mild white fish, about 8 ounces
1	teaspoon margarine, melted
1	tablespoon reduced-sodium soy sauce
1	tablespoon lemon juice
$1/2$	teaspoon Worcestershire sauce
$1/2$	teaspoon ground ginger
1	garlic clove, minced
$1/8$	teaspoon grated lemon peel
$1/8$	teaspoon freshly ground black pepper
$1/2$	tablespoon sugar

Parsley sprigs for garnish

Lemon wedges for garnish

Linguine and Clam Sauce

An impressive dish that's quick and easy to prepare.

3	garlic cloves, minced
2	tablespoons minced onion
2	tablespoons olive oil
1	cup white wine
2	cups canned clams and juice
$1/8$	teaspoon white pepper
8	ounces linguine
2	tablespoons chopped fresh parsley
$1/4$	cup grated Parmesan cheese

In a large saucepan over medium-high heat, sauté the garlic and onion in the oil. Add the wine. Reduce the heat to low and simmer for 30 minutes. Add the clams with juice and pepper; simmer for about 10 minutes. While the clams are simmering, cook the linguine according to package directions; drain well. Put the linguine in a large shallow serving bowl and spoon clam sauce over. Sprinkle with the parsley. Serve immediately and pass Parmesan cheese to accompany.

Yield: 4 servings

1 serving contains: *Cal 346kc, Prot 17gm, Fat 11gm, Chol 62mg, Carb 38gm, Fib 1gm, Sodium 165mg*

Salmon Soy Steak

Rinse the fish and pat dry. Combine the soy sauce and garlic powder in a zip-lock plastic bag. Add the salmon, turning the bag to coat well. Marinate in the refrigerator for 3 to 12 hours.

Preheat the oven to broil. Remove the salmon from the soy sauce marinade; discard the mixture and place salmon on a broiler pan. Combine the olive oil and lemon juice, brush over salmon; sprinkle with salt and pepper. Broil for 5 minutes. Lower the oven temperature to 425°F (220°C). Sprinkle the lemon zest over fish; bake, covered for 15 minutes or until the salmon flakes easily.

Yield: 4 servings

1 serving contains: *Cal 341kc, Prot 39gm, Fat 18gm, Chol 105mg, Carb 4gm, Fib 0, Sodium 1230mg*

$1/2$ cup reduced-sodium soy sauce

2 teaspoons garlic powder

$1^1/2$ pounds salmon fillets

Freshly ground black pepper to taste

1 tablespoon olive oil

Zest and juice of 1 lemon

Sweet and Sour Salmon

1½ pounds salmon fillets

½ cup orange juice

¼ cup balsamic vinegar

2 teaspoons brown spicy mustard

2 teaspoons olive oil

2 teaspoons finely chopped fresh basil*

2 teaspoons finely chopped fresh mint*

Sprigs of fresh basil or mint for garnish

Preheat the oven to 425°F (220°C); spray a small baking pan with vegetable spray. Rinse the fish, pat dry, and place in prepared baking pan. In a small bowl combine the orange juice, vinegar, mustard, oil, basil, and mint; pour over the fish; cover with foil. Bake for 13 to 15 minutes or until the fish flakes when tested with a fork. Serve the remaining juices with the fish. Garnish with fresh basil or mint sprigs.

Yield: 4 servings

* If fresh basil or mint is not available, use 1 teaspoon dried.

1 serving contains: *Cal 321kc, Prot 37gm, Fat 17gm, Chol 105mg, Carb 4gm, Fib 0, Sodium 112mg*

Crab Quiche

Read the label to make sure the imitation crab ingredients are allowed in your diet.

Preheat the oven to 400°F (205°C). Prick the piecrust and bake for 4 minutes; prick again and bake 5 minutes longer. While the crust is baking, combine the remaining ingredients in a large bowl. Pour into the piecrust and bake for 30 to 40 minutes or until set. Let stand 10 minutes before serving.

Yield: 6 servings

1 serving contains: *Cal 296kc, Prot 15gm, Fat 15gm, Chol 14mg, Carb 25gm, Fib 1gm, Sodium 574mg*

1	(9-inch) uncooked Piecrust, page 302
2	egg whites
1/2	cup egg substitute
1/2	cup evaporated skim milk
1/2	cup shredded reduced-fat Swiss cheese
2	tablespoons chopped onion
1/4	teaspoon salt
1/4	teaspoon dried marjoram
1/4	teaspoon lemon pepper
8	ounces steamed fresh or imitation crab, cut into bite-size pieces

Salmon Patties

An old favorite that is low in fat and cholesterol.

1   (15½-ounce) can salmon

¼ cup chopped onion

½ teaspoon prepared
     mustard

About 1 cup fine cracker
crumbs*

2   egg whites

½ cup all-purpose flour

1   teaspoon canola oil

Juice from one fresh lemon

Dill or parsley for garnish

Drain the salmon, reserving the broth. In a large bowl, combine the salmon, onion, mustard, crumbs, egg whites, flour, and enough broth to moisten. Add more cracker crumbs or broth if needed to make patties firm. Flour your hands and make 4 patties; roll patties in additional flour. Heat the oil in a medium-size nonstick skillet over medium heat. Add the patties and cook on both sides until browned. Drizzle with fresh lemon juice and garnish with fresh dill or parsley. Serve immediately.

Yield: 4 servings

* Substitute ¼ cup oat bran for ¼ cup cracker crumbs.

1 serving contains: *Cal 281kc, Prot 26gm, Fat 9gm, Chol 47mg, Carb 20gm, Fib 1gm, Sodium 742mg*

Tilapia

Peppers and tomatoes add great color to this fish.

Rinse the fish, pat dry, set aside. Heat 1 tablespoon of the olive oil in a nonstick skillet. Add the peppers and onion; sauté until tender. Add the garlic, stir, and cook for about 1 minute more. Remove from the skillet, set aside. Add the remaining olive oil to the skillet. Place fish in hot oil and sauté until fish flakes with a fork. Season with salt, pepper, and dill. Spoon the veggies over the fish in skillet. Add the tomatoes and wine; cook for 3 to 4 minutes more.

Yield: 4 servings

1 serving contains: *Cal 289kc, Prot 44gm, Fat 8gm, Chol 109mg, Carb 6gm, Fib 1gm, Sodium 263mg*

2	pounds tilapia or other mild, white fish
$1^1/2$	tablespoons olive oil, divided
$1/2$	green bell pepper, sliced
$1/2$	red bell pepper, sliced
1	tablespoon porcini peppers, chopped
$1/2$	medium onion, sliced
4	garlic cloves, minced
Salt and pepper to taste	
$1/2$	teaspoon dill
16	cherry tomatoes
$1/2$	cup dry white wine

Crabmeat-Topped Potatoes

Great for a light meal.

6 ounces steamed fresh or canned crabmeat, drained
1 tablespoon olive oil
$^{1}/_{4}$ cup chopped green pepper
$^{1}/_{4}$ cup chopped green onions
1 garlic clove, minced
1 (8-ounce) package reduced-fat cream cheese, softened
$^{1}/_{4}$ cup skim milk
$^{1}/_{2}$ cup reduced-fat sour cream
$^{1}/_{2}$ teaspoon freshly ground pepper
4 large baking potatoes, baked*

Prepare the crabmeat as needed. Heat the olive oil in a medium skillet. Add the green pepper and onions; sauté until tender. Add the garlic; stir for about 2 minutes. Remove from the heat. Add the cream cheese to the vegetable mixture, stirring until smooth. Add the milk and sour cream; stir until blended. Return to low heat just until heated through. Add the crabmeat and pepper. Cut the potatoes length wise, open slightly, sprinkle with salt. Spoon the crabmeat mixture over top and serve immediately.

Yield: 4 servings

❋ For a nice crisp shell, pierce potato several times and lightly rub vegetable oil over the potatoes. Place potatoes directly on the rack in a 400°F oven for 1 hour or until potato gives when pressed.

Note: **This is great served with Cabbage Salad, page 100.**

1 serving contains: *Cal 430kc, Prot 23gm, Fat 18gm, Chol 87mg, Carb 46gm, Fib 4gm, Sodium 381mg*

Sautéed Scallops

Arrange around a bed of rice.

Melt the margarine in a large nonstick skillet over medium-high heat. Add the celery, green onion, and garlic; sauté until wilted. Add the scallops, wine, basil, lemon pepper, and parsley. Cook over medium-high heat for about 5 minutes or until tender, stirring often but gently. With a slotted spoon, remove the scallops and vegetables to a plate. Add the mayonnaise to skillet, blending with wine mixture. Return the scallops and vegetables to the skillet and toss gently to coat. Garnish with parsley. Serve immediately.

Yield: 4 ($^3/_4$-cup) servings

1 serving contains: *Cal 177kc, Prot 29gm, Fat 3gm, Chol 57mg, Carb 6gm, Fib trace, Sodium 326mg*

2	teaspoons margarine or butter
$^1/_4$	cup finely chopped celery
3	tablespoons finely chopped green onion
2	garlic cloves, minced
$1^1/_2$	pounds bay scallops, rinsed, drained well
3	tablespoons white wine
$^1/_2$	teaspoon dried basil
$^1/_4$	teaspoon lemon pepper
1	tablespoon chopped fresh parsley plus more for garnish
2	tablespoons reduced-fat mayonnaise

Baked Scallops with Tarragon

Looks impressive and is quick and easy to prepare.

1	cup white wine
1	tablespoon chopped fresh parsley
1/4	teaspoon dried tarragon
3	peppercorns
1	pound bay scallops or ocean scallops, cut into quarters
1 1/2	tablespoons all-purpose flour
2	tablespoons cornstarch
2/3	cup evaporated skim milk
1	teaspoon lemon juice
1 1/2	tablespoons chopped pimiento
1	teaspoon butter or margarine
4	teaspoons grated Parmesan cheese
Parsley sprigs for garnish	

Preheat the oven to 350°F (175°C). In a saucepan, combine the wine, parsley, tarragon, and peppercorns. Bring to a boil; reduce the heat and simmer for 5 minutes. Add the scallops and return to a boil. Reduce the heat to medium; cook until the scallops are tender and look opaque. Remove the scallops from the broth; set aside. In a jar with a lid, combine the flour, cornstarch, and milk; shake until dissolved. Gradually add to the simmering broth, stirring constantly until the broth thickens and starts to bubble. Cook for 1 minute; add the scallops, lemon juice, pimiento, and margarine; toss to coat well. Spray 4 individual baking dishes or a shallow 1-quart baking dish with cooking spray. Spoon the scallops and sauce into prepared dishes. Sprinkle with the Parmesan cheese. Bake for 10 minutes or until bubbling and beginning to brown. Garnish with parsley sprigs. Serve immediately.

Yield: 4 servings

1 serving contains: *Cal 213kc, Prot 24gm, Fat 2gm, Chol 41mg, Carb 14gm, Fib trace, Sodium 286mg*

Steamed Fish in Foil

Flavorful, moist way to prepare fish.

Preheat the oven to 375°F (190°C). Rinse the fish and pat dry. In a small bowl, blend the remaining ingredients, except garnish, and stir to a creamy mixture. Lay a piece of heavy-duty aluminum foil large enough to wrap two pieces of fish on a working surface. Lay one fillet on the foil. Spread with a portion of creamed mixture, then top with a second fillet. Fold the foil over the fish and tightly seal the edges. Place in a medium-size baking dish. Prepare the remaining fillets in the same manner. Bake for 15 to 20 minutes or until the fish flakes easily. Remove from the foil, being careful to save juices. Garnish with cilantro or parsley sprigs and lemon wedges. Serve immediately.

Yield: 3 servings

6 fillets white fish, about 1 pound

2 tablespoons margarine, softened

$1/2$ teaspoon brown mustard

1 tablespoon snipped chives

Pepper to taste

1 teaspoon lemon juice

1 small garlic clove, minced

Cilantro or parsley sprigs, lemon wedges for garnish

1 serving contains: *Cal 178kc, Prot 29gm, Fat 6gm, Chol 73mg, Carb 2gm, Fib trace, Sodium 228mg*

Grilled Salmon

Serve with fresh corn cooked on the grill.

Top the salmon with Cucumber Sauce, page 237.

2	salmon steaks, about $3/4$ pound
1	teaspoon margarine or butter, melted
1	teaspoon lemon juice
$1/4$	teaspoon dill weed
$1/4$	teaspoon garlic powder
$1/4$	teaspoon lemon pepper

Rinse the fish and pat dry. In a small bowl, combine the margarine, lemon juice, dill, garlic powder, and lemon pepper. Place the salmon in a shallow dish and pour the margarine mixture over the salmon; refrigerate at least 30 minutes. Heat a grill or broiler. Lightly brush the grill rack with oil. Place the salmon on grill rack for 4 to 5 minutes, basting occasionally with juices. Turn the steaks and continue basting until the fish flakes easily, about 4 minutes, depending on the thickness of steaks, or until internal temperature reads 135°F. Serve immediately.

Yield: 2 servings

1 serving contains: *Cal 289kc, Prot 43gm, Fat 14gm, Chol 77mg, Carb 1gm, Fib 0, Sodium 116mg*

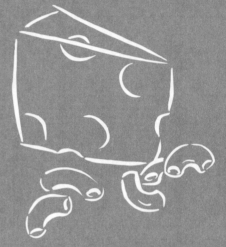

Meatless
Meals

On days when your family feels like a change from poultry and seafood, feed them a meatless meal. They contribute nutrition, color, and variety to your menu without high fat and cholesterol.

It is possible to get plenty of protein in vegetarian or meatless meals. Protein sources in these meatless recipes include beans, eggs, milk, and cheese. Additionally, foods like beans, vegetables, and whole grains are great sources of fiber and are naturally low in fat.

Many foods that typically contain meat can be made meatless (i.e., Vegetarian Lasagna, page 193, and Vegetarian Pizza, page 194). There is no end to the vegetable combinations you can use to top this delicious homemade pizza crust. Try something new each time you make it. Keep your family interested in their "no red meat" diet! Another favorite of ours is spaghetti with marinara sauce, served with grated Parmesan cheese.

Bean Enchiladas

Try a mild variety of picante sauce the first time you make this dish.

1   recipe Refried Beans, page 208, omit cheese

2   ounces diced canned green chilies

4   cups picante sauce, divided

10 large flour tortillas

1   cup shredded reduced-fat Cheddar cheese, divided

Shredded lettuce for garnish

Chopped green onion for garnish

Diced tomatoes for garnish

Picante sauce for garnish

Preheat the oven to 350°F (175°C). In a large iron skillet or heavy saucepan, stir the beans and green chilies over low heat until warm. Pour 1/4 cup of the picante sauce into a large shallow dish. Dip 1 tortilla in sauce, coating both sides. Remove to a plate. Spoon 1/4 to 1/3 cup of beans at 1 edge of tortilla; sprinkle a little cheese over the beans and fold over. Pour 1/4 cup of the picante sauce in the bottom of a large shallow casserole and lay the enchiladas in the sauce as you make them. When all the enchiladas are made, pour the remaining picante sauce over all. Bake, covered, for 30 minutes. Uncover, sprinkle the remaining cheese on top, and bake for 5 minutes longer. Serve immediately garnished as desired.

Yield: 5 (2-enchilada) servings

1 serving contains: *Cal 709kc, Prot 35gm, Fat 12gm, Chol 16mg, Carb 121gm, Fib 11gm, Sodium 1686mg*

Tomato-Onion Pizza

Preheat the oven to 425°F (220°C). Place the pizza crust in a pan. Sauté the onions and garlic in 1 tablespoon of the olive oil. Toss the tomatoes in remaining olive oil with salt and pepper. Spread the onions and garlic over the crust; scatter tomatoes over the onions. Bake for about 20 minutes or until the crust is browned. Sprinkle with basil and oregano.

Yield: 3 servings

* Use the dough for Vegetarian Pizza on page 194, or when I am in a hurry I use a reduced-fat pizza crust or a reduced-fat focaccia found in the bakery section of your grocery.

1 serving contains: *Cal 337kc, Prot 9gm, Fat 13gm, Chol 0, Carb 50gm, Fib 7gm, Sodium 497mg*

1	(12-inch) reduced-fat pizza crust*
1	medium onion, thinly sliced
4	garlic cloves, cut into slivers
2	tablespoons extra-virgin olive oil, divided
2	cups grape or cherry tomatoes, cut in half

Dash of salt

Freshly ground black pepper

3	tablespoons chopped fresh basil or 1 1/2 tablespoons dried
1	teaspoon fresh oregano or 1/2 teaspoon dried

Eggplant Mozzarella

A great meal, low in all the "no-no's."

$\frac{1}{2}$ cup chopped green onion

$\frac{1}{2}$ cup sliced fresh mushrooms

$\frac{1}{4}$ cup water

2 cups spaghetti sauce

$\frac{1}{2}$ teaspoon salt

1 small eggplant, peeled, sliced

1 egg white, slightly beaten

1 tablespoon water

$\frac{1}{2}$ cup all-purpose flour

1 teaspoon olive oil

1 cup reduced-fat cottage cheese

1 cup (4-ounces) shredded part-skim mozzarella cheese

Preheat the oven to 350°F (175°C). In a large saucepan over low heat, cook the green onion and mushrooms in the water until tender. Add the spaghetti sauce; bring to a boil. Reduce the heat; simmer 20 to 25 minutes. Sprinkle the salt over the sliced eggplant; set aside to drain about 10 minutes. In a shallow bowl, beat the egg white and water together. Dip the eggplant in the egg mixture, then into the flour. In a large nonstick skillet, heat a few drops of oil over medium heat. Add the eggplant slices and cook until browned, turning once; drain on a paper towel. Continue until all slices are cooked. In a 13 x 9-inch casserole, spread about $\frac{1}{2}$ cup sauce. Add a layer of eggplant, top with $\frac{1}{2}$ cup cottage cheese and more sauce. Repeat until all ingredients are used, ending with sauce. Sprinkle with the mozzarella cheese. Bake, uncovered, for 30 minutes. Let stand 5 minutes before serving.

Yield: 9 servings

Variation:

✦ **For an exceptionally nutritious dish, add slices of tofu between the layers.**

1 serving contains: *Cal 152kc, Prot 9gm, Fat 6gm, Chol 8mg, Carb 17gm, Fib 1gm, Sodium 551mg*

Enchilada-Bean Bake

Add nachos and salsa to complete this meal.

Preheat the oven to 350°F (175°C). In a large iron skillet or any large heavy skillet over low heat, cook the garlic, onion, and mushrooms in the water until tender. Add the beans, tomatoes, wine, chili powder, and cumin. Heat over medium-high heat until boiling; reduce the heat and simmer for about 30 minutes or until most of the liquid is gone. Using a potato masher, thoroughly mash the beans. In a small bowl, mix the cottage cheese and yogurt; set aside. In a medium-size shallow casserole, put a layer of tortillas, a layer of beans, and a little cottage cheese mixture. Continue to layer until all ingredients are used, ending with cottage cheese mixture. Sprinkle with Cheddar cheese. Bake, uncovered, for about 30 minutes or until bubbling. Serve immediately garnished with shredded lettuce and chopped green onion.

Yield: 6 servings

1 serving contains: *Cal 193kc, Prot 12gm, Fat 3gm, Chol 5mg, Carb 29gm, Fib 5gm, Sodium 327mg*

2	garlic cloves, minced
1/3	cup finely chopped onion
1/2	cup chopped fresh mushrooms
1/4	cup water
2	cups cooked beans, navy or pintos
1 1/2	cups stewed tomatoes
1/2	cup red wine
1	teaspoon chili powder or to taste
1	teaspoon ground cumin
1/2	cup reduced-fat cottage cheese
1/4	cup plain reduced-fat yogurt
1/4	cup shredded reduced-fat Cheddar cheese
4 to 5	corn tortillas

Shredded lettuce for garnish

Chopped green onion for garnish

Stacked Mexican Quiche

Easy and delicious for breakfast, lunch, or dinner.

4   (6-inch) corn tortillas

3   tablespoons all-purpose flour

1/2 teaspoon garlic powder

1/4 teaspoon chili powder

1/4 teaspoon salt

1   cup thinly sliced yellow squash (1 medium)

1   cup chopped tomato

1/3 cup thinly sliced green onions

1/4 cup mild salsa

1/2 cup egg substitute

2   egg whites

1/2 cup evaporated skim milk

Freshly ground pepper

1/2 cup (2 ounces) shredded, reduced-fat Mexican three cheese blend*

Preheat the oven to 350°F (175°C). Spray a 9-inch pie pan with vegetable spray; arrange the tortillas around the pie plate. In a shallow dish combine the flour, garlic powder, chili powder, and salt; dredge the squash in the flour mixture, reserve the remaining flour mixture. Arrange the squash over the tortillas; top with the tomato and onions. Sprinkle the reserved flour mixture over the vegetables, spoon the salsa evenly over all. Combine the egg substitute, egg whites, and milk; pour over the vegetables, sprinkle with the pepper. Be careful to cover edges of tortillas to prevent over baking. Bake, uncovered, for 25 minutes or until a knife comes out clean. Top with cheese; bake for 5 minutes more or until cheese is melted. Let stand 5 minutes before cutting.

Yield 4 servings

∗ Can substitute sharp Cheddar cheese.

1 serving contains: *Cal 194kc, Prot 14mg, Fat 7mg, Chol 16mg, Carb 21 gm, Fib 2gm, Sodium 454mg*

Macaroni and Cheese

New approach to an old favorite.

Preheat the oven to 350°F (175°C). In a large saucepan, cook the macaroni in boiling water with the onion and rosemary, if desired, according to package directions or about 8 minutes. Drain, discarding the onion and rosemary; set aside. Put 1½ cups milk in a medium-size saucepan over medium heat. In a jar with a lid, combine the remaining ½ cup milk, flour, and powdered milk; shake until completely dissolved. Slowly add to the warm milk in the saucepan, stirring constantly, until the mixture begins to thicken. Cover about 1 minute, stirring constantly. Set aside 2 tablespoons of the cheese. Add the remaining cheese, margarine, salt, and pepper to the sauce; stir until the cheese is melted. Pour the sauce over macaroni and toss gently to coat well. Spoon into a deep 2-quart casserole. Sprinkle the reserved cheese over all. Sprinkle lightly with parsley. Bake, uncovered, for 10 minutes or until the cheese melts.

Yield: 6 (½-cup) servings

1 serving contains: *Cal 151kc, Prot 10gm, Fat 4gm, Chol 12mg, Carb 20gm, Fib trace, Sodium 335mg*

1	cup elbow macaroni
1	small onion, peeled, cut in half
1	sprig fresh rosemary, optional
2	cups skim milk, divided
2	tablespoons all-purpose flour
1	tablespoon nonfat powdered milk
½	cup (2 ounces) shredded reduced-fat American cheese, divided
1	teaspoon margarine or butter
¼	teaspoon salt
Pepper to taste	
2	teaspoons chopped fresh parsley

Lasagna-Spinach Rings

Add a green salad and crusty bread for a complete dinner.

10 lasagna noodles

1 (10-ounce) package thawed frozen chopped spinach

$1/4$ cup minced onion

2 tablespoons grated Parmesan cheese

1 cup reduced-fat cottage cheese

$1/8$ teaspoon pepper

Dash of ground nutmeg

3 cups spaghetti sauce

Preheat the oven to 350°F (175°C). Cook the noodles according to package directions; drain. Drain the spinach thoroughly, then squeeze in a paper towel. In a medium-size bowl, combine the spinach, onion, cheeses, pepper, and nutmeg. On a clean working surface, lay a noodle out flat. Spread the spinach mixture evenly along the noodle, then roll up jelly-roll fashion and secure with a wooden pick. Continue until all ingredients are used. In a medium-size casserole, pour a little spaghetti sauce to cover bottom of dish; stand the prepared noodles in the sauce. Pour the remaining sauce over noodles. Sprinkle lightly with nutmeg. Bake, uncovered, for 25 to 30 minutes or until the sauce is bubbling. Serve immediately.

Yield: 5 (2-noodle) servings

1 serving contains: *Cal 359kc, Prot 16gm, Fat 9gm, Chol 4mg, Carb 56gm, Fib 2gm, Sodium 1021mg*

Vegetarian Lasagna

Make two: one to eat now and one to freeze.

In a medium-size saucepan, combine the carrots, broccoli, spinach, onion, and all of the seasonings. Add just enough water to prevent the mixture from sticking. Simmer 30 minutes or until all the liquid is absorbed. Meanwhile, cook the lasagna noodles according to package directions. Drain and quickly rinse in cold water to stop cooking; drain again and set aside. Preheat the oven to 350°F (175°C). Reserve 2 cups of the mozzarella cheese. In a small bowl, mix the cottage cheese, the remaining mozzarella, the Parmesan and egg whites; set aside. Pour about ½ cup of the spaghetti sauce into a large lasagna pan. Place a layer of noodles over sauce; add layers of vegetables, cottage cheese mixture, and sauce. Continue layering until all ingredients are used, ending with sauce. Sprinkle the remaining mozzarella over the top. Bake, uncovered, for 1 hour. Let stand for 10 minutes before cutting.

Yield: 12 servings

1 serving contains: *Cal 348kc, Prot 23gm, Fat 11gm, Chol 27mg, Carb 40gm, Fib 2gm, Sodium 810mg*

2	carrots, shredded, about 2 cups
1	cup bite-size broccoli pieces
1	(10-ounce) package frozen chopped spinach, thawed and well drained
1	cup chopped onion
1	teaspoon garlic powder
½	teaspoon dried basil
1	teaspoon dried oregano
1	tablespoon chopped fresh parsley
½	teaspoon seasoned salt
1	(16-ounce) box lasagna noodles
4	cups (1 pound) shredded part-skim mozzarella cheese, divided
2	cups reduced-fat cottage cheese
½	cup grated Parmesan cheese
2	egg whites, slightly beaten
3	cups spaghetti sauce, divided

Vegetarian Pizza

What a treat—have your pizza and eat it too!

Dough:

1   ($1/4$-ounce) package active dry yeast
1   cup warm water (110°F, 45°C)
1   tablespoon sugar
1   teaspoon salt
1   tablespoon plus 1 teaspoon canola oil, divided
$1^1/2$ cups whole wheat flour
1   cup unbleached all-purpose flour, divided
1   teaspoon cornmeal

Topping:

$1^3/4$ cups pizza sauce
1   medium onion, cut into rings, separated
1   green bell pepper, thinly sliced
7 to 8   fresh mushrooms, sliced
3   cups (12 ounces) shredded reduced-fat mozzarella cheese
2   tablespoons grated Parmesan cheese

In a mixing bowl, dissolve the yeast in the water. Add the sugar, salt, 1 tablespoon oil, whole wheat flour, and ½ cup all-purpose flour; mix well. Knead in mixer with a dough hook for 2 minutes on low speed. Gradually add the remaining flour until dough comes away from sides of bowl. Knead on low speed about 7 minutes or until the dough is smooth and elastic, or knead by hand. With 1 teaspoon oil, grease a large bowl and two (12-inch) pizza pans. Lightly sprinkle the cornmeal over the pans. Put the dough in the greased bowl; cover, and let rise in a warm place until doubled in bulk, about 1 hour. Punch down the dough. Divide the dough in half; press each half in bottom and up sides of each pan. Cover and let rise in a warm place for 20 minutes. Preheat the oven to 425°F (220°C). Spread the sauce over the dough. Arrange the onion, green pepper, and mushrooms over sauce. Crumble the mozzarella cheese over the vegetables and sprinkle with the Parmesan cheese. Bake for 20 minutes or until browned and bubbling.

Yield: 6 (2-wedge) servings

1 serving contains: *Cal 466kc, Prot 24gm, Fat 17gm, Chol 34mg, Carb 57gm, Fib 5gm, Sodium 995mg*

Vegetarian Stuffed Peppers

Subtle flavor blending makes these delicious!
Red or yellow bell peppers can also be used.

Cut the tops off the peppers; remove and discard the seeds. Place the peppers in a large saucepan. Add water to cover and cook over medium-high heat about 5 minutes or until crisp-tender; invert over a paper towel to drain well. While the peppers are cooking, combine the onion, garlic, rice, apple, corn, bread-crumbs, dill, tarragon, paprika, and pepper in a medium-size bowl. Set pepper upright in a deep 8-inch square baking dish and spoon equal amounts of stuffing into each one. Preheat the oven to 350°F (175°C).

For the topping, in a small bowl, combine the breadcrumbs, margarine, and cheese. Spoon over top of each stuffed pepper; sprinkle with paprika. Bake for 40 to 45 minutes. Serve immediately.

Yield: 4 servings

1 serving contains: *Cal 376kc, Prot 12gm, Fat 5gm, Chol 8mg, Carb 76gm, Fib 3gm, Sodium 686mg*

4	green bell peppers
1/2	cup finely chopped onion
2	garlic cloves, minced
1	cup cooked long-grain white rice
1	cup finely chopped apple
2	cups creamed corn
1/3	cup fresh breadcrumbs
1/4	teaspoon dill weed
1/4	teaspoon dried tarragon
1/2	teaspoon paprika
Freshly ground black pepper to taste	

Topping:

1/2	cup fresh breadcrumbs
1	teaspoon margarine, melted
1/2	cup shredded reduced-fat American cheese
Dash of paprika	

Vegetable Tostadas

Serve this for a delightful, light lunch.

Add Refried Beans, page 208, for a heartier meal.

1   small onion,
     thinly sliced

1/4 cup thinly sliced celery

1/4 cup chopped green
     bell pepper

1/2 cup water

2   large zucchini, thinly
     sliced, about 1 pound

4 to 5   fresh mushrooms,
     sliced, about 1 cup

1/4 teaspoon salt

4   corn tortillas, warmed

1   cup (4 ounces)
     shredded reduced-fat
     Cheddar cheese

1/2 cup plain reduced-fat
     sour cream

2   tomatoes, chopped, about
     1 1/4 cups

1/4 cup salsa

In a large nonstick skillet over medium-high heat, cook the onion, celery, and green pepper in the water for 3 to 4 minutes or until tender. Add the zucchini, mushrooms, and salt; cook for about 4 minutes longer or until the vegetables are crisp-tender; drain well. Lay warm tortillas on a baking sheet; divide the vegetable mixture evenly over the tortillas. Sprinkle with shredded cheese. Place in a 350°F (175°C) oven for 3 to 5 minutes or until cheese melts. Top with sour cream, tomatoes, and salsa. Serve immediately.

Yield: 2 (2-tostada) servings

1 serving contains: *Cal 419kc, Prot 28gm, Fat 15gm, Chol 44mg, Carb 50gm, Fib 8gm, Sodium 952mg*

Vegetables and Rice

Vegetables play a very important role in our meals. They provide vitamins, minerals, and fiber, while at the same time adding color and flavor.

Always choose the freshest possible vegetables. Use them as close as possible to the time of purchase. This may mean shopping for produce twice a week, but the nutritional results are worth the extra trip to the store. Always wash vegetables well just prior to cooking. Cook with skins on if possible; precious vitamins are lost with the peelings. Use a small amount of water so the water-soluble vitamins are retained. The most important point to remember about cooking vegetables is not to overcook. Cook just until barely tender.

Herbs and spices add zest to all vegetables. Take advantage of the wide variety of herbs available today. I eliminate salt by using herbs. Use herbs sparingly at first, then experiment with increased amounts. See the herb section, pages 16–19.

I like to liven up steamed green beans with a touch of margarine and a sprinkling of dill weed or tarragon. Fresh chopped or dried basil works well with crisp-tender carrots. A small amount of reduced-fat shredded cheese also gives a tasty touch to simply cooked vegetables. My family enjoys broccoli dusted with grated Parmesan cheese. Halved tomatoes broiled with a little cheese and basil on top make an appealing side dish with poached fish. Next time you plan an outdoor get-together, put some of your favorite vegetables such as zucchini, yellow squash, cherry tomatoes, mushrooms, or onion wedges on skewers. They can be brushed with a little oil from time to time or basted with your favorite barbecue sauce.

We enjoy the nutty flavor of brown rice, and hope you'll try it too. Brown Rice Pilaf is a great basic dish. You can personalize it by adding your favorite spices and vegetables.

Hopping John, page 206, is a traditional Southern dish, combing rice and black-eyed peas.

Green Beans with Walnuts

Crunchy walnuts make a difference.

2   pounds fresh green beans
3   tablespoons butter*
1/2 cup chopped walnuts
1/4 teaspoon salt
Freshly ground pepper to taste

Wash the beans; trim and cut them into bite-size pieces. Place in medium saucepan, add a small amount of water, bring to a slow boil, and reduce the heat to medium low; continue to cook until crisp-tender. Drain, immediately turn into a bowl filled with ice water for 1 minute; drain again and set aside.

In large nonstick skillet melt the butter, add the walnuts, and cook for about 5 minutes, continuing to stir. Add the beans, tossing to coat with butter, and add salt and pepper; cover partially and cook, tossing and stirring occasionally about 6 minutes or until heated through.

Yield: 10 servings

* Substitute olive oil if desired.

1 serving contains: *Cal 106kc, Prot 3gm, Fat 7gm, Chol 12mg, Carb 7gm, Fib 3gm, Sodium 64mg*

Green Beans and Dill

Dill makes it different!

Put about ½ cup water into a medium-size saucepan. Add the beans and cook over medium-low heat until nearly tender. Add the mushrooms and cook 1 minute longer. Drain and add pimiento, olive oil, and dill; toss gently to mix. Remove from the heat. Cover and let stand for a few minutes before serving. To serve, garnish with lemon peel, if desired.

Yield: 4 (½-cup) servings

1 serving contains: *Cal 29kc, Prot 1gm, Fat 1gm, Chol 0, Carb 6gm, Fib 1gm, Sodium 14mg*

2 cups prepared fresh or frozen green beans

2 tablespoons sliced fresh mushrooms

2 tablespoons chopped pimiento

1 teaspoon extra-virgin olive oil

½ teaspoon dill weed

Strips of lemon peel for garnish, optional

Spanish Lima Beans

A colorful combination dish.

1	cup frozen lima beans
1/2	cup water
1	tablespoon chopped onion
1/2	bay leaf
1/2	cup fresh or frozen whole kernel corn
1/2	cup chopped fresh or canned tomatoes
1/4	teaspoon dried marjoram
1	teaspoon margarine*
1/4	teaspoon salt
Pepper to taste	

Put the beans, water, onion, and bay leaf into a medium-size saucepan; cook for about 10 minutes over medium heat. Add the corn, tomatoes, marjoram, margarine, salt, and pepper; cook for about 15 minutes longer or until lima beans are tender. Drain and serve immediately.

Yield: 3 (1/2-cup) servings

* You can substitute extra-virgin olive oil.

1 serving contains: *Cal 94kc, Prot 5gm, Fat 1gm, Chol 0, Carb 18gm, Fib 4gm, Sodium 275mg*

Candied Acorn Squash

Use "lite" maple syrup because it has half the calories of regular syrup.

2	acorn squash
4	tablespoons "lite" maple syrup, divided
2	teaspoons margarine or butter, divided
1/8	teaspoon ground allspice

Preheat the oven to 375°F (190°C). Wash the squash and cut in half; remove the seeds and stringy parts. Place the squash halves, cut side up, in a medium-size shallow baking dish. Put 1 tablespoon syrup and ½ teaspoon margarine in each half; dust with allspice. Bake, covered, for 35 minutes, then uncover and bake for about 15 minutes longer or until tender. Serve immediately.

Yield: 4 servings

1 serving contains: *Cal 125kc, Prot 2gm, Fat 1gm, Chol 0, Carb 30gm, Fib 3gm, Sodium 30mg*

Scalloped Turnips

You'll be proud to take this casserole anywhere.

1 pound turnips, about 3 small

1/2 cup skim milk

1 teaspoon margarine

1/4 cup shredded reduced-fat American cheese

1/2 cup fresh breadcrumbs

Dash of ground ginger

1/8 teaspoon salt

Dash of pepper

1 tablespoon grated Parmesan cheese

Peel and slice turnips. Put in a medium-size saucepan and add water to cover. Bring to a boil, then reduce the heat. Cover and simmer for 12 to 15 minutes or just until tender; drain well. Preheat the oven to 350°F (175°C). While the turnips are cooking, heat the milk and margarine in a small saucepan. When hot, but not boiling, quickly stir in the American cheese until melted. Add the breadcrumbs, ginger, salt, and pepper. Pour over the turnips, tossing gently to coat well. Spoon into a 1-quart casserole and sprinkle with Parmesan cheese. Bake for 15 minutes, then put under preheated broiler until top is browned. Serve immediately.

Yield: 4 (1/2-cup) servings

1 serving contains: *Cal 107kc, Prot 6gm, Fat 3gm, Chol 6mg, Carb 16gm, Fib 1gm, Sodium 336mg*

Brown Rice Pilaf

Brown rice retains the original nutrients of the rice kernel.
The nutty flavor complements chicken or seafood dishes.

P reheat the oven to 350°F (175°C). In a medium-size saucepan over medium heat, cook the onion in 2 tablespoons water until tender. Add the rice and stir constantly until heated. Stir in the chicken broth, 1 cup water, and sage; bring to a boil. Pour into a 2-quart ovenproof casserole. Bake, covered, for 50 to 60 minutes or until liquid is absorbed and rice is tender. Fluff with a fork before serving.

Yield: 6 (^{1}/2-cup) servings

2	tablespoons chopped onion
2	tablespoons plus 1 cup water
1	cup brown rice
2	cups reduced-fat, reduced-sodium chicken broth
^{1}/4	teaspoon rubbed sage

Variation:

✦ **Sherried Brown Rice Pilaf:** Omit sage. Cook 1/2 cup sliced fresh mushrooms with onion. Combine with rice and bake as directed. When done, stir in 3 tablespoons sherry.

1 serving contains: *Cal 130kc, Prot 4gm, Fat 1gm, Chol trace, Carb 25gm, Fib 3gm, Sodium 259mg*

Hopping John

This Southern favorite brings good luck when eaten on New Year's Day. Top with spicy salsa.

$^1/_2$ cup chopped red and green bell pepper

$^1/_2$ cup chopped onion

$^1/_4$ cup water

6 cups cooked black-eyed peas

2 cups cooked long-grain rice

$^1/_4$ teaspoon red (cayenne) pepper or to taste

$^1/_2$ teaspoon salt

In a large saucepan over low heat, cook the bell peppers and onion in water until tender. Stir in the peas, rice, and red pepper. Season with the salt. Cook over low heat until most of the liquid is absorbed. Serve immediately.

Yield: 16 ($^1/_2$-cup) servings

1 serving contains: *Cal 98kc, Prot 6gm, Fat 1gm, Chol 0, Carb 18gm, Fib trace, Sodium 76mg*

Slow-Baked Beans

Great for a picnic.

Preheat the oven to 350°F (175°C). Combine the beans, catsup, brown sugar, onion, tomatoes, and bell pepper in a 3-quart casserole. Bake, covered, for 2½ hours. If the beans have too much liquid, remove the lid for the final 30 minutes of cooking; stir occasionally. Serve hot or warm.

Yield: 3 (½-cup) servings

1 serving contains: *Cal 121kc, Prot 5gm, Fat trace, Chol 0, Carb 25gm, Fib 4gm, Sodium 75mg*

3	cups cooked pinto beans
3	cups cooked lima beans
¼	cup catsup
3	tablespoons firmly packed brown sugar
½	cup chopped onion
2	large fresh tomatoes, cut into eighths, about 2½ cups
1	cup chopped green bell pepper

Refried Beans

Perfect side dish with Chicken Fajitas, page 150.

Sprinkle with ½ cup shredded low-fat Cheddar cheese for extra flavor.

2	tablespoons olive oil
¼	cup chopped onion
1	garlic clove, minced
1	cup cooked tomatoes, seeds removed
¼	cup diced green chilies
½	cup white wine
¼	teaspoon chili powder
1	teaspoon ground cumin
6	cups cooked pinto beans

In a large soup kettle heat the olive oil over low heat, add the onion and garlic, cook until brown. Add the tomatoes, chilies, wine, chili powder, cumin, and beans; bring to a boil. Reduce the heat to medium low and simmer for about 45 minutes. Heat a large, deep iron skillet or any large, heavy skillet over medium low. With a slotted spoon, lift some beans out of liquid and put into the skillet. Mash with a potato masher, keeping the beans in constant motion. Continue adding and mashing the remaining beans. Serve immediately.

Yield: 10 (½-cup) servings

1 serving contains: *Cal 97kc, Prot 4gm, Fat 7gm, Chol trace, Carb 13gm, Fib 2gm, Sodium 60mg*

Red Cabbage

Good make-ahead side dish that's even more delicious the second day.

In a heavy skillet, heat the oil over medium-high heat. Add the onion and sauté until tender. Add the cabbage, apple, cloves, and bay leaf. Cover and simmer for about 20 minutes or until the cabbage is tender. If the cabbage gets dry, add a small amount of water. Add the sugar and vinegar to the cabbage mixture; toss gently. Cover and cook for about 5 minutes longer. Serve immediately.

Yield: 6 ($^3/_4$-cup) servings

1 serving contains: *Cal 45kc, Prot 1gm, Fat 1gm, Chol 0, Carb 9gm, Fib 2gm, Sodium 5mg*

1	teaspoon canola oil
$^1/_2$	cup finely chopped onion
4	cups coarsely shredded red cabbage, about $^1/_2$ head
1	cup chopped peeled apple
2	whole cloves
$^1/_2$	bay leaf
1	tablespoon brown sugar
$1^1/_2$	tablespoons white vinegar

Gingered Carrots

Colorful for a special dinner.

6	medium-size carrots, peeled, cut into 1-inch pieces
1	tablespoon sugar
1	teaspoon cornstarch
$1/8$	teaspoon ground nutmeg
$1/4$	teaspoon ground ginger
$1/4$	cup orange juice
1	teaspoon margarine or butter

Steam the carrots just until tender; drain. While the carrots are cooking, combine the sugar, cornstarch, nutmeg, and ginger in a small saucepan; add the orange juice. Cook over medium heat, stirring constantly, until the sauce thickens. Cook for 1 minute, then remove from the heat and stir in the margarine. Place the carrots in a serving dish; pour the sauce over them, tossing to coat evenly. Cover and let stand 4 to 5 minutes before serving.

Yield: 6 ($1/2$-cup) servings

1 serving contains: *Cal 52kc, Prot 1gm, Fat 1gm, Chol 0, Carb 12gm, Fib 3gm, Sodium 60mg*

Oven-Roasted Red Potatoes, Peppers, and Patty Pan Squash

Roasting brings out the flavor in vegetables.

Preheat the oven to 425°F (220°C). Wash and dry all the vegetables; cut into chunks. Place all the vegetables in a zip-lock plastic bag; add the olive oil; seal and shake to coat. Place in a baking pan and roast, uncovered, for 40 to 45 minutes or until tender, stirring occasionally. Season with salt and pepper, and garnish with fresh herbs.

Yield: 4 servings

1 serving contains: *Cal 240kc Prot 5gm, Fat 7gm, Chol 0, Carb 41gm, Fib 4gm, Sodium 87mg*

5	small red potatoes
1	Patty Pan squash
1	red bell pepper
1	green bell pepper
1	small onion
2	tablespoons extra-virgin olive oil
1/8	teaspoon sea salt

Freshly ground black pepper to taste

Any fresh herbs for garnish

Corn and Zucchini Casserole

Prepare ahead. When ready to serve pop into the oven until cheese melts.

1 tablespoon extra-virgin olive oil or less

¼ cup chopped onion

1 garlic clove, minced

3 small zucchini, thinly sliced, about 2 cups

3 ears fresh corn cut from cob, about 2 cups kernels*

Freshly ground pepper to taste

2 tablespoons fresh basil

¼ cup shredded part-skim mozzarella cheese

Heat the olive oil in a large nonstick skillet over medium-high heat; when hot, add the onion and sauté until tender. Add the garlic and cook for about 30 seconds, stirring constantly to prevent garlic from getting too brown. Add the zucchini and sauté for about 4 minutes; add the corn; continue to cook for 2 to 3 minutes until the zucchini is tender. Add the pepper and basil and then spoon into prepared casserole; top with cheese and heat in the oven until the cheese is melted.

Yield: 4 servings

* Can use frozen or thawed corn.

1 serving contains: *Cal 122kc, Prot 5gm, Fat 6gm, Chol 4mg, Carb 16gm, Fib 3gm, Sodium 54mg*

Zippy Cauliflower

Green chilies and cheese pack it with flavor.

Preheat the oven to 350°F (175°C). Steam the cauliflower just until tender; drain. Melt the margarine in a medium-size saucepan over medium heat. In a jar with a lid, combine the flour, red pepper, salt, pepper, and milk; shake until blended. Slowly add to the margarine in the saucepan, stirring constantly until smooth. Add the cheese and continue stirring until smooth and slightly thickened. Stir in the chilies. Arrange the cauliflower in a 2-quart baking dish; pour the sauce over the cauliflower, then sprinkle with the breadcrumbs. Bake for 10 to 15 minutes or until bubbling. Serve immediately.

Yield: 6 (1/2-cup) servings

1 serving contains: *Cal 73kc, Prot 5gm, Fat 2gm, Chol 7mg, Carb 9gm, Fib 1gm, Sodium 209mg*

3	cups cauliflower, florets and some stems
1/2	teaspoon margarine
1	tablespoon all-purpose flour
1/8	teaspoon red (cayenne) pepper
1/4	teaspoon salt
1/8	teaspoon pepper
3/4	cup skim milk
1/2	cup shredded reduced-fat Cheddar cheese
2	tablespoons chopped green chilies
1/4	cup fresh breadcrumbs

Sautéed Zucchini, Squash, Onion, and Tomato

Yummy fresh vegetables.

$1/2$ tablespoon extra-virgin olive oil

2 medium zucchini, sliced

2 medium yellow squash, sliced

1 small onion, cut into wedges

1 garlic clove, minced

1 large fresh tomato, chopped or 1 small can crushed tomatoes

$1/8$ teaspoon sea salt

Freshly ground pepper

1 tablespoon fresh basil, chopped, or 1 teaspoon dried

Heat the oil in a nonstick skillet; sauté the squash and onion for 4 to 5 minutes. Add the garlic and continue to cook for about 1 minute. Add the chopped tomato; cook until all is tender. Season with salt, pepper, and basil.

Yield: 6 servings

1 serving contains: *Cal 37kc, Prot 2gm, Fat 1gm, Chol 0, Carb 6gm, Fib 2, Sodium 57*

Potato Cakes

Always a favorite with children.

In a medium-size bowl, combine the potatoes, egg white, onion, flour, salt, and pepper. Heat the oil in a large skillet over medium-high heat. When hot, put about 2 tablespoons potato mixture for each cake into the skillet. Cook until well browned, then turn with a spatula and cook the other side until brown. Continue making cakes with the remaining mixture, keeping first ones warm. Serve immediately.

Yield: 6 (3-inch-cake) servings

1 serving contains: *Cal 74kc, Prot 2gm, Fat 1gm, Chol 1mg, Carb 15gm, Fib trace, Sodium 260mg*

2	cups mashed potatoes
1	egg white, slightly beaten
2	tablespoons chopped onion
2	tablespoons all-purpose flour
1/8	teaspoon salt
Pepper to taste	
1	teaspoon canola oil

Potato-Cheese Puff

Potato casserole with a unique flavor.

2   **cups mashed potatoes**
1   **tablespoon minced onion**
2   **tablespoons skim milk**
1   **cup reduced-fat cottage cheese**
1/2 **teaspoon margarine or butter**
Paprika to taste

Preheat the oven to 350°F (175°C). In a medium-size bowl, combine the potatoes, onion, milk, cottage cheese, and margarine. Spoon into a 1-quart casserole; sprinkle with the paprika. Bake, uncovered, for 25 minutes or until beginning to brown. Serve immediately.

Yield: 5 (1/2-cup) servings

1 serving contains: *Cal 114kc, Prot 7gm, Fat 2gm, Chol 2mg, Carb 18gm, Fib 1gm, Sodium 193mg*

Summer Squash Medley

This is my very favorite way of cooking delicious summer squash.

Slice the squash into medium slices; cut the onion into wedges. Heat the olive oil in a nonstick skillet; add the squash, onion, and garlic. Sauté until just crisp-tender. Season with lemon juice, pepper, and chives.

Yield: 4 servings

* Balsamic vinegar is very nice with these vegetables instead of the lemon juice.

1 serving contains: *Cal 49kc, Prot 2gm, Fat 3gm, Chol 0, Carb 7 gm, Fib 1gm, Sodium 6mg*

1 medium yellow squash

1 medium zucchini

2 medium Patty Pan squash

2 teaspoons extra-virgin olive oil

1/2 small onion

1 garlic clove, minced

2 teaspoons fresh lemon juice*

Freshly ground black pepper

2 tablespoons fresh chives, chopped

Pennsylvania Sweet Potatoes in Tangy Sauce

Different sweet potatoes for your holiday menu.

6	large sweet potatoes, scrubbed
1	cup granulated sugar
1/2	cup lightly packed brown sugar
1/4	teaspoon ground ginger
2	tablespoons cornstarch
1	cup unsweetened pineapple juice
1	teaspoon lemon juice
1	tablespoon margarine or butter

Place the sweet potatoes in a large kettle and add water to cover. Cook over medium heat until barely tender; drain. Peel and cut the potatoes into fourths. Arrange in a medium-size casserole. Preheat the oven to 350°F (175°C). While the potatoes are cooking, combine the sugars, ginger, and cornstarch in a small saucepan. Add the pineapple juice and lemon juice. Stir over medium heat until the sugars are dissolved and the mixture starts to bubble; stir in the margarine. Pour the sauce over the potatoes. Bake, uncovered, for 50 to 60 minutes or until the sauce is thickened. Serve immediately.

Yield: 10 (1/2-cup) servings

1 serving contains: *Cal 149kc, Prot 1gm, Fat trace, Chol 0, Carb 37gm, Fib 1gm, Sodium 18mg*

Oven French Fries

So much better than the old greasy kind.

Preheat the oven to 350°F (175°C). Peel the potatoes and slice for French fries. Lay them out on several layers of paper towel to absorb moisture; pat dry with another paper towel. The potatoes should be as dry as possible. Put the potatoes in a large bowl and drizzle with the oil, tossing to coat evenly. Lay them in a single layer on a large baking sheet; sprinkle the dry dressing mix and parsley over all. Bake for 25 minutes, then turn them over; only do this once. Return to the oven and increase the temperature to 450°F (230°C). Cook for 3 to 5 minutes longer or until the potatoes are tender and start to brown. Serve immediately.

Yield: 4 servings

1 serving contains: *Cal 239kc, Prot 4gm, Fat 7gm, Chol 0, Carb 42gm, Fib 2gm, Sodium 256mg*

6   medium potatoes, washed, about 3 pounds

2   tablespoons canola oil

1   (1-ounce) package Good Seasons Italian Dressing, not mixed

1   tablespoon chopped fresh parsley

Brown Rice

Keep small portions in your freezer to add to other dishes.

2   **tablespoons finely chopped onion**

2   **teaspoons canola or olive oil**

2   **cups water or broth**

1   **cup uncooked long-grain brown rice**

In a medium-size saucepan over low heat, cook the onion in oil until tender. Add the rice, stirring until heated; add the water. Cover and bring to a boil. Reduce the heat to low and simmer for about 1 hour or until all liquid is absorbed and rice is tender. Fluff with a fork before serving.

Yield: 6 (^{1}/$_2$-cup) servings

1 serving contains: *Cal 124kc, Prot 2gm, Fat 2gm, Chol 0, Carb 25gm, Fib 3gm, Sodium trace*

Rice and Green Onion

A green rice casserole.

Preheat the oven to 350°F (175°C). In a medium-size saucepan, sauté the green onion and green pepper in oil over medium heat. Add the rice, parsley, broth, and pepper; bring to a boil. Pour into a 2-quart casserole. Bake, covered, for 20 minutes or until all the liquid is absorbed and the rice is tender. Fluff with a fork before serving.

Yield: 6 (^{1}/$_2$-cup) servings

1 serving contains: *Cal 139kc, Prot 4gm, Fat 1gm, Chol 0, Carb 27gm, Fib 1gm, Sodium 265mg*

^{3}/$_4$ cup thinly sliced
green onion

^{1}/$_2$ cup chopped green
bell pepper

1 teaspoon canola
or olive oil

1 cup uncooked
long-grain brown rice

^{1}/$_4$ cup chopped
fresh parsley

2 cups hot reduced-fat,
reduced-sodium
chicken broth

Pepper to taste

221

Rice and Pecan Pilaf

Pecans are optional, depending on your diet limitations.

1	teaspoon margarine or butter, divided
1/2	cup chopped pecans
1/4	cup chopped onion
1	cup uncooked long-grain white rice
2	cups hot reduced-fat, reduced-sodium chicken broth
1/8	teaspoon dried thyme
1/8	teaspoon pepper
1	tablespoon chopped fresh parsley

Preheat the oven to 350°F (175°C). Melt 1/2 teaspoon margarine in a medium-size skillet over medium-high heat. Add the pecans and sauté for about 2 minutes. Remove from the skillet and set aside. Melt the remaining 1/2 teaspoon margarine in the skillet; add the onion and sauté until tender. Add the rice and stir to coat. Add the chicken broth, thyme, pepper, and parsley. Cover and bring to a boil. Pour into a 2-quart casserole. Bake, uncovered, for 17 minutes or until all the liquid is absorbed and rice is tender. Just before serving, stir in the pecans and fluff with a fork.

Yield: 6 (1/2-cup) servings

Variation:

✦ **Stove-Top Rice and Pecan Pilaf:** Cook on top of the stove in the skillet by simmering, covered, for 18 to 20 minutes.

1 serving contains: *Cal 190kc, Prot 4gm, Fat 7gm, Chol trace, Carb 27gm, Fib 1gm, Sodium 268mg*

Lou's Grilled Vegetables

Make ahead for your cookout.

Preheat the grill to medium hot. Divide the potatoes, carrots, onions, and zucchini among 6 large pieces of heavy-duty aluminum foil. Put 4 cherry tomatoes, then 1/4 teaspoon margarine on each stack. Add the salt and pepper. Fold the foil over several times to seal tightly. The vegetables can be made a few hours ahead to this point and refrigerated. Place the foil packages on the grill and cook for about 30 minutes, turning occasionally, until vegetables are tender. Serve immediately.

Yield: 6 servings

1 serving contains: *Cal 162kc, Prot 4gm, Fat 1gm, Chol 0, Carb 36gm, Fib 7gm, Sodium 123mg*

4	potatoes, scrubbed, thinly sliced, about 3 cups
4	carrots, thinly sliced, slightly cooked, about 3 cups
2	onions, cut into rings, about 2 cups
2	zucchini, medium sliced, about 2 cups
24	cherry tomatoes, cut in half
1 1/2	teaspoons margarine
1/4	teaspoon salt
Pepper to taste	

Grilled Asparagus

Clean, fresh flavor.

1   pound asparagus

1   teaspoon extra-virgin olive oil

1   teaspoon lemon juice

Freshly ground white pepper

Heat the grill to medium. Spray the grill rack with olive oil spray. Rinse the asparagus, break off tough ends, and lay on paper towel to drain. Arrange the asparagus on a baking sheet and brush with olive oil. Arrange the asparagus spears on the grill rack; cook over the hot coals for about 5 minutes or until crisp-tender. Place in serving bowl and sprinkle lemon juice and pepper before serving.

Yield: 4 servings

1 serving contains: *Cal 38kc, Prot 3gm, Fat 1gm, Chol 0, Carb 5gm, Fib 2gm, Sodium 2mg*

Stir-Fried Vegetables

Enhances any meal.

Heat a wok or a large nonstick skillet over medium-high heat; add the oil and heat. Stir-fry the garlic and ginger in the oil for about 5 seconds. Add the vegetables and stir-fry quickly for about 1 minute to coat with oil. Stir-fry about 2 minutes longer. Add water to the pan; cover and steam for 2 to 3 minutes. Stir in the soy sauce. In a small bowl, blend the cornstarch and broth. Pour over the vegetables and cook for about 30 seconds longer or until sauce thickens. Serve immediately.

Yield: 7 (^{1}/2-cup) servings

1 serving contains: *Cal 45kc, Prot 2gm, Fat 2gm, Chol trace, Carb 5gm, Fib 1gm, Sodium 364mg*

1	tablespoon canola oil
1	garlic clove, minced
1	thin slice fresh ginger root, minced
4	cups prepared fresh raw vegetables*
2 to 3	tablespoons water
2	tablespoons reduced-sodium soy sauce
1	tablespoon cornstarch
^{1}/2	cup reduced-fat, reduced-sodium chicken broth

* Suggested vegetables:

Asparagus
cut into 2-inch pieces

Bell peppers
cut into chunks

Broccoli
cut into florets, stems sliced

Cabbage
coarsely sliced

Carrots
thinly sliced

Cauliflower
cut into florets

Celery
thinly sliced diagonally

Green beans
cut into 2-inch pieces

Mushrooms
thickly sliced

Onion
sliced

Snow peas
whole

Water chestnuts
medium sliced

Zucchini
medium sliced

Tomato Slices with Herbs

A wonderful summer treat.

3 medium-size tomatoes,
   about 1 pound

²/₃ cup fresh breadcrumbs

1 tablespoon margarine,
   melted

¹/₄ teaspoon dried basil

Preheat the oven to 350°F (175°C). Slice the tomatoes and arrange them in a medium-size shallow baking dish. Put the breadcrumbs in a small bowl and stir in the margarine and basil. Sprinkle the breadcrumb mixture over the tomatoes. Bake, uncovered, for 5 to 6 minutes or until the breadcrumbs are brown. Serve immediately.

Yield: 6 servings

1 serving contains: *Cal 65kc, Prot 2gm, Fat 2gm, Chol 0, Carb 11gm, Fib 1gm, Sodium 109mg*

Quick Parmesan Couscous

Parmesan cheese adds new flavor.

Bring the broth and butter to a boil. Stir in the couscous, cover, and remove from the heat. Let stand for 5 minutes. Stir in the Parmesan cheese, lemon juice, and olive oil; fluff with fork. Add the pepper and serve immediately.

Yield: 4 servings

1 serving contains: *Cal 328kc, Prot 12gm, Fat 8gm, Chol 12mg, Carb 51gm, Fib 3gm, Sodium 569mg*

2	cups reduced-fat, reduced-sodium chicken broth
2	teaspoons butter
1	(10-ounce) package plain couscous
$1/3$	cup grated Parmesan cheese
1	tablespoon fresh lemon juice
1	tablespoon extra-virgin olive oil
$1/4$	teaspoon salt
	Freshly ground black pepper

Stuffed Zucchini

A pretty dish that goes together quickly.

2   medium-size zucchini, about 1 pound

1   tablespoon olive oil

3   tablespoons finely chopped fresh mushrooms

1   tablespoon finely chopped onion

1   tablespoon finely chopped green bell pepper

1/2   teaspoon dried basil

1/4   teaspoon dried oregano

2   tablespoons fresh breadcrumbs

1   cup tomato sauce

1   tablespoon shredded reduced-fat Cheddar cheese

Preheat the oven to 350°F (175°C). Rinse the zucchini; cut lengthwise into halves. Scoop out the centers and finely chop the pulp. Put the chicken broth into a medium-size nonstick skillet over medium-high heat. Add the zucchini pulp, mushrooms, onion, green pepper, basil, and oregano; cook until limp. Remove from the heat. Add the breadcrumbs and toss well. Add more broth if needed to make stuffing stick together. Fill the zucchini shells with stuffing. Pour a little tomato sauce into a shallow medium-size baking dish. Place the stuffed zucchini in the dish and pour the remaining tomato sauce over all. Bake, uncovered, for 25 to 30 minutes; sprinkle with cheese and bake for 5 minutes longer. Serve immediately.

Yield: 4 servings

1 serving contains: *Cal 92kc, Prot 4gm, Fat 4gm, Chol 1mg, Carb 11gm, Fib 2gm, Sodium 106mg*

Greens, Turnips, and Sweet Potato

Great dish, high fiber, low fat.

Wash the greens thoroughly, let drain; stack several on top of each other cut into approximately 1 to 2-inch slices, set aside.

Bring the broth to a boil in a medium soup pot; add the onion and sweet potato. Cover and cook for 4 to 5 minutes. Stir in the carrots and turnips; cover and cook for 8 to 10 minutes or until just starting to get tender. Add the greens, salt, and pepper; cover and cook until the greens are just wilted. Sprinkle with Parmesan cheese before serving.

Yield: 8 servings

* When purchasing greens, whether at the market or your farm stand, they will be sold in a bunch.

1 serving contains: *Cal 73kc, Prot 5gm, Fat 2gm, Chol 6mg, Carb 10gm, Fib 3gm, Sodium 427*

1	bunch of greens of your choice, chard, turnip, mustard, etc.*
1	(15-ounce) can reduced-fat, reduced-sodium vegetable broth
1	medium onion, sliced
1	medium sweet potato, peeled and sliced
2	carrots, peeled and cut into chunks
6	small turnips or 1 large cut into chunks
$1/2$	teaspoon salt
Freshly ground black pepper	
$1/2$	cup Parmesan cheese

229

Southwest Zucchini Casserole

Zucchini, chilies, and cheese are a real Tucson treat.

4	small zucchini, about 1 1/4 pounds
1/2	cup minced onion
1/2	cup minced celery
1/4	cup water
1/4	cup diced green chilies
Salt and pepper to taste	
1/2	cup shredded reduced-fat Cheddar cheese

Rinse the zucchini; cut lengthwise into fourths, then cut into pieces. Steam the zucchini until crisp-tender. In a small saucepan over low heat, cook the onion and celery in the water until tender. Preheat the broiler. Put the zucchini in a 2-quart casserole and add the onion, celery, green chilies, salt, and pepper; toss gently to combine. Sprinkle the cheese over top and place under the broiler just until the cheese is melted and starting to brown. Serve immediately.

Yield: 5 (1/2-cup) servings

1 serving contains: *Cal 57kc, Prot 5gm, Fat 2gm, Chol 8mg, Carb 6gm, Fib 2gm, Sodium 97mg*

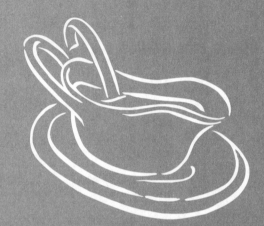

Sauces
and Gravies

Sauces and gravies add a totally new dimension to the most mundane foods. Here is a wide variety of sauces to complement many dishes—from Cheese Sauce, page 236, for vegetables or entrees to Chocolate Sauce, page 249, for an otherwise plain low-fat white cake.

Always use low-fat ingredients and stir well. For a cooked sauce or gravy, use a heavy saucepan to help prevent sticking.

Some recipes can be frozen, such as Grandma's Barbecue Sauce, Marinara Sauce, and Tomato Sauce. Other sauces like Herb Margarine and Chocolate Sauce will keep in the refrigerator for several days and can be used as needed.

While these sauces are much lower in fat, cholesterol, and calories than traditional recipes, they must still be used with discretion. Always take into consideration your total fat, cholesterol, and calories for the day. Plan your menu accordingly.

Chicken Milk Gravy

No need to add salt if you use canned broth or seasoned homemade broth.

$2^{1}/_{2}$ tablespoons cornstarch

$^{1}/_{4}$ cup nonfat
powdered milk

2 cups reduced-fat,
reduced-sodium
chicken broth

Pepper to taste

In a medium-size saucepan, thoroughly blend the cornstarch and powdered milk; gradually stir in the broth. Cook over medium-high heat, stirring constantly, until the mixture thickens. Season with pepper before serving.

Yield: 2 cups or 8 ($^{1}/_{4}$-cup) servings

1 serving contains: *Cal 26kc, Prot 2gm, Fat trace, Chol 1mg, Carb 4gm, Fib 0, Sodium 206mg*

Chicken Gravy

Use your own unsalted homemade broth and the sodium content will be much lower than given below.

In a cup, thoroughly blend a small amount of the broth and cornstarch. Add to the remaining broth in a medium-size saucepan. Cook over medium-high heat, stirring constantly, until the gravy thickens. Season with pepper before serving.

Yield: 2 cups or 8 ($^1/_4$-cup) servings

2 cups reduced-fat, reduced-sodium chicken broth

$2^1/_2$ tablespoons cornstarch

Pepper to taste

1 serving contains: *Cal 19kc, Prot 1gm, Fat trace, Chol trace, Carb 2gm, Fib 0, Sodium 194mg*

Cheese Sauce

A real treat to serve over steamed vegetables.

1	tablespoon margarine
1/4	teaspoon salt
1/8	teaspoon pepper
1/4	teaspoon dry mustard
3/4	cup skim milk
1	tablespoon all-purpose flour
1/2	cup shredded reduced-fat American or Cheddar cheese

In a small heavy saucepan, melt the margarine over medium heat; add the salt, pepper, and dry mustard. In a small jar with a lid, combine the milk and flour; shake well until blended. Slowly stir the milk mixture into the margarine in the saucepan. Add the cheese and cook over medium heat, stirring constantly, until the sauce has thickened slightly.

Yield: 1 1/2 cups or 10 (2-tablespoon) servings

1 serving contains: *Cal 31kc, Prot 2gm, Fat 2gm, Chol 7mg, Carb 2gm, Fib trace, Sodium 117mg*

Cucumber Sauce for Fish

Clean, fresh flavor for your favorite fish.

In a small bowl, combine the cucumber, sour cream, mayonnaise, dill weed, lemon juice, and pepper. Cover and refrigerate for 1 to 2 hours. Bring the sauce close to room temperature shortly before serving. When the fish is ready to serve, gently place on a serving platter and spoon sauce over fish.

Yield: 1 1/2 cups or 12 (2-tablespoon) servings

1 serving contains: *Cal 39kc, Prot 1gm, Fat 3gm, Chol 9mg, Carb 2gm, Fib trace, Sodium 28mg*

1	medium cucumber, peeled, shredded
1	cup reduced-fat sour cream
2	tablespoons reduced-fat mayonnaise
1	teaspoon dill weed
1	teaspoon lemon juice
Pepper to taste	

Caper Sauce

Creamy caper sauce perks up your fish recipes.

$^1/_2$ cup reduced-fat
sour cream

2 tablespoons
drained capers

$^1/_4$ teaspoon
brown mustard

$^1/_2$ teaspoon lemon juice

In a small bowl, blend the sour cream, capers, mustard, and lemon juice. Cover and refrigerate for 1 to 2 hours. Bring the sauce close to room temperature shortly before serving. When the fish is ready to serve, gently place on a serving platter and spoon the sauce over the fish.

Yield: $^3/_4$ cup or 6 (2-tablespoon) servings

1 serving contains: *Cal 16kc, Prot 2gm, Fat trace, Chol 1mg, Carb 1gm, Fib trace, Sodium 81mg*

Tomato Sauce

When tomatoes are in season, freeze to use later as a base for sauces such as Marinara Sauce, page 243.

Mark the tomatoes with a small X at the non-blossom end, then put in boiling water for 1 minute. Plunge the tomatoes into iced water for 1 minute, then peel. Cut into quarters and put in a medium-size saucepan with the onion and garlic. Bring to a boil; reduce the heat to low and simmer uncovered, until the vegetables are tender. Put the vegetables through a food mill, or purée in a blender or food processor fitted with the metal blade; strain to remove the seeds. Return the puréed mixture to the saucepan with herbs. Cook over low heat for 1 to 2 hours or until thickened. Use in chicken or pasta dishes or serve warm with poached fish.

2	pounds fresh tomatoes
2	tablespoons finely chopped onion
1	garlic clove, chopped
1	tablespoon minced fresh parsley
1	teaspoon dried basil or dill weed

Yield: About 3$\frac{1}{2}$ cups or 7 ($\frac{1}{2}$-cup) servings

1 serving contains: *Cal 28kc, Prot 1gm, Fat trace, Chol 0, Carb 6gm, Fib 2gm, Sodium 11mg*

Grandma's Barbecue Sauce

Always a favorite basting sauce for family get-togethers.

2	cups stewed tomatoes
1/2	cup water
1/2	cup catsup
1/2	cup Worcestershire sauce
1	cup finely chopped onion
1	garlic clove, minced
1/2	cup vinegar
1	tablespoon sugar
1/8	teaspoon red (cayenne) pepper
1/8	teaspoon black pepper
1/4	teaspoon dry mustard
2	teaspoons margarine

Put the tomatoes through a food mill or process in a food processor fitted with a metal blade; strain the seeds. Put the strained tomatoes, water, catsup, Worcestershire sauce, onion, garlic, vinegar, and sugar into a medium-size saucepan. Cook, covered, over medium-high heat until boiling. Reduce the heat to low and add the red pepper, black pepper, and dry mustard. Simmer, uncovered, until the sauce starts to thicken. Add the margarine and stir until blended. Taste and adjust seasoning, if necessary. Serve as desired.

Yield: 2 cups or 16 (2-tablespoon) servings

1 serving contains: *Cal 32kc, Prot 1gm, Fat trace, Chol 0, Carb 7gm, Fib trace, Sodium 239mg*

Buttery Herb Sauce

Keep some in the refrigerator at all times. Spoon over chicken or fish before baking. It's delicious over savory filled crêpes and most steamed or baked vegetables.

In a small saucepan, melt the butter over medium heat. Stir in the garlic, parsley, thyme, and pepper. Remove from the heat; cover, and let stand for 4 to 5 minutes. Store in the refrigerator and melt before using.

Yield: 4 (1-tablespoon) servings

1 serving contains: *Cal 39kc, Prot trace, Fat 4gm, Chol 0, Carb trace, Fib trace, Sodium 105mg*

3	tablespoons butter
1	garlic clove, minced
1	tablespoon chopped fresh parsley
$1/2$	teaspoon dried thyme
$1/8$	teaspoon pepper

Basic White Sauce

Used in numerous dishes as a base for other sauces or to bind mixtures. Makes a good low-salt substitute for undiluted canned cream soup.

2 tablespoons all-purpose flour

1 tablespoon nonfat powdered milk

1 cup skim milk

$^1/_8$ teaspoon salt

$^1/_8$ teaspoon white pepper

1 tablespoon butter

In a jar with a lid, combine the flour, powdered milk, and skim milk; shake until completely dissolved. Pour into a medium-size saucepan and cook over medium heat, stirring constantly, until the sauce thickens. Stir in the salt, pepper, and butter.

Yield: 1 cup or 4 ($^1/_4$-cup) servings

Variations:

✦ **Thin White Sauce:** Using the recipe above, reduce flour to 1 tablespoon.

✦ **Mushroom Sauce:** Add $^1/_2$ cup chopped fresh sautéed mushrooms.

✦ **Tomato Sauce:** Stir in $^1/_4$ cup tomato paste.

✦ **Celery Sauce:** Add 2 tablespoons finely chopped sautéed celery and $^1/_2$ teaspoon celery salt.

✦ **Chicken Sauce:** Add 1 teaspoon chicken bouillon granules.

1 serving contains: *Cal 63kc, Prot 3gm, Fat 3gm, Chol 9mg, Carb 7gm, Fib trace, Sodium 125mg*

Marinara Sauce

Keep an extra batch in the freezer.

In a large cast-iron skillet or soup pot over medium-high heat, cook the garlic, onion, and green pepper in $1/4$ cup water until tender. Pour into a food processor fitted with the metal blade or a food mill. Add the tomatoes and process until puréed; strain the tomato seeds. Return the vegetable purée to the skillet or pot. Add the tomato sauce, tomato paste, remaining $1\frac{1}{2}$ cups water, Italian seasoning, basil, oregano, sugar, allspice, parsley, salt, and pepper; cover and bring to a boil. Reduce the heat to a simmer. Simmer, uncovered, for about 2 hours or until the sauce reaches desired thickness. Taste and adjust the seasoning, if necessary. Spoon over chicken or fish before or after baking or broiling. Serve as a sauce with pasta.

Yield: 2 cups or 8 ($1/4$-cup) servings

1 serving contains: *Cal 43kc, Prot 2gm, Fat trace, Chol 0, Carb 10gm, Fib 1gm, Sodium 313mg*

3	garlic cloves, minced
1	cup chopped onion
$3/4$	cup chopped green bell pepper
$1^{3}/4$	cups water, divided
1	(28-ounce) can crushed Italian tomatoes
1	(8-ounce) can tomato sauce
1	(6-ounce) can tomato paste
$1^{1}/2$	teaspoons Italian seasoning
1	teaspoon dried basil
$1/2$	teaspoon dried oregano
3	teaspoons sugar
$1/8$	teaspoon ground allspice
1	tablespoon chopped fresh parsley
$1/2$	teaspoon salt
$1/8$	teaspoon pepper

Mornay Sauce

Smooth, flavorful, and almost no fat.

1	cup skim milk
2	tablespoons nonfat powdered milk
2	tablespoons all-purpose flour
1/4	teaspoon salt
1/4	cup grated Parmesan cheese
1	teaspoon lemon juice

In a jar with a lid, combine the skim milk, powdered milk, flour, and salt; shake until completely dissolved. Pour into a small heavy saucepan. Cook over medium heat, stirring constantly, until the sauce thickens; cook for 2 minutes longer. Remove from the heat and stir in the cheese and lemon juice. Serve hot with vegetables or fish.

Yield: 1 1/2 cups or 12 (2-tablespoon) servings

1 serving contains: *Cal 24kc, Prot 2gm, Fat 1gm, Chol 2mg, Carb 2gm, Fib trace, Sodium 94mg*

Judy's Mushroom Sauce

Splendid over chicken or vegetables.

In a medium-size heavy saucepan, melt the margarine over medium-high heat. Add the mushrooms and sauté until tender. Reduce the heat to medium. In a jar with a lid, combine the flour and milk; shake until completely dissolved. Slowly add to the mushrooms, stirring constantly. Cook for 3 or 4 minutes, stirring frequently. Add the soy sauce. Stir constantly until the sauce thickens. Season with pepper. Spoon over baked chicken or poached fish.

Yield: 1 1/4 cups or 10 (2-tablespoon) servings

1 serving contains: *Cal 39kc, Prot 2gm, Fat 2gm, Chol 1mg, Carb 3gm, Fib trace, Sodium 68mg*

2	tablespoons margarine or butter
1/2	cup sliced fresh mushrooms or 1 (4-ounce) can
1	tablespoon all-purpose flour
3/4	cup evaporated skim milk
1	teaspoon reduced-sodium soy sauce

White pepper to taste

Orange Sauce

For a special dessert, serve with Apple Crêpes, page 309.

$^1/_2$ cup sugar

1 teaspoon cornstarch

$^1/_2$ cup orange juice

$^1/_4$ teaspoon grated orange peel

1 tablespoon margarine or butter

1 tablespoon orange liqueur

In a small saucepan, thoroughly combine the sugar and cornstarch. Add the orange juice and cook over medium heat, stirring constantly until the sauce starts to thicken. Add the orange peel, margarine, and liqueur; stir until blended. Serve warm with your dessert of choice.

Yield: $^3/_4$ cup or 6 (2-tablespoon) servings

1 serving contains: *Cal 87kc, Prot trace, Fat 1gm, Chol 0, Carb 20gm, Fib trace, Sodium 24mg*

Strawberry Sauce

Add a special touch to Strawberry Crêpes, page 310.

In a small saucepan, thoroughly combine the sugar and cornstarch. Gradually stir in the water, lemon juice, and crushed strawberries. Stir over medium heat until boiling; cook for about 3 minutes longer, then set aside to cool. The sauce will thicken as it cools. Serve at desired temperature with dessert of choice.

Yield: 1 1/4 cups or 10 (2-tablespoon) servings

1 serving contains: *Cal 85kc, Prot trace, Fat trace, Chol 0, Carb 22gm, Fib trace, Sodium trace*

1	cup sugar
3 1/2	tablespoons cornstarch
1/2	cup water
1	teaspoon lemon juice
1/2	cup crushed strawberries

Tart Lemon Sauce

Perks up any dish.

2 tablespoons margarine or butter
1 tablespoon lemon juice
1 tablespoon chopped fresh parsley

In a small saucepan, melt the margarine over medium heat. Stir in the lemon juice and parsley. Remove from heat; cover and let stand 4 to 5 minutes. Spoon over cooked fish or steamed vegetables.

Yield: 4 (1-tablespoon) servings

1 serving contains: *Cal 26kc, Prot trace, Fat 3gm, Chol 0, Carb trace, Fib trace, Sodium 70mg*

Chocolate Sauce

Delicious served as a fondue with fresh fruit or as a topping over Angel food cake.

In a medium-size saucepan, mix the sugar and cocoa well. Add the milk and margarine; bring to a boil over medium-high heat, stirring constantly. Reduce the heat to medium and cook for 5 minutes longer, stirring frequently. Remove from the heat. Add the vanilla and beat vigorously for 1 minute. Stir vigorously from time to time as the sauce cools. Serve warm.

Yield: $2^1/_3$ cups or 18 (2-tablespoon) servings

1 serving contains: *Cal 110kc, Prot 2gm, Fat 1gm, Chol 2mg, Carb 25gm, Fib 0, Sodium 32mg*

2	cups sugar
7	tablespoons unsweetened cocoa
$1^2/_3$	cups evaporated skim milk
$1^1/_2$	teaspoons margarine or butter
1	teaspoon vanilla extract

Vanilla Sauce

Finishing touch for Dutch Apple Cake, page 266.

$1/4$ cup sugar

$1^1/2$ teaspoons cornstarch

$1/8$ teaspoon ground nutmeg

$1/2$ cup boiling water

$1/2$ tablespoon margarine or butter

1 teaspoon vanilla extract

In a small saucepan, thoroughly combine the sugar, cornstarch, and nutmeg. Slowly stir in the boiling water and cook, stirring, over medium heat until the sauce thickens; cook for 1 minute longer. Remove from the heat and stir in the margarine and vanilla. Serve warm with your dessert of choice.

Yield: $3/4$ cup or 6 (2-tablespoon) servings

1 serving contains: *Cal 38kc, Prot trace, Fat 1gm, Chol 2mg, Carb 9gm, Fib 0, Sodium 19mg*

Lemon-Raisin Sauce

One of our family's favorites served over Gingerbread, page 274, or Dutch Apple Cake, page 266.

I n a small saucepan, blend the sugar and cornstarch. Gradually add the water, stirring constantly over medium heat until boiling; boil for 1 minute. Remove from the heat and stir in the lemon juice, margarine, and raisins. Serve warm with your dessert of choice.

Yield: 9 (3-tablespoon) servings

1 serving contains: *Cal 74kc, Prot trace, Fat trace, Chol 1mg, Carb 18gm, Fib 1gm, Sodium 11mg*

1/2	cup sugar
1	tablespoon cornstarch
1	cup boiling water
2	tablespoons lemon juice
1	teaspoon margarine or butter
1/2	cup raisins

Sandwiches

When preparing sandwiches for your family or friends, be creative! Make the food as interesting and appealing as possible. Use a wide variety of breads as the base for your sandwiches. Alternate among whole wheat, rye, pumpernickel, sourdough, pita bread, English muffins, and tortillas. Homemade Biscuits, page 67, are delicious when filled with your favorite chicken or tuna salad. Don't forget the wide assortment of crisp flatbreads, rice cakes, and crackers. Always read labels to make sure the crackers are acceptable to your new way of eating.

What could be simpler for a nutritious sandwich than taking a small flour tortilla and adding a slice of reduced-fat cheese? Toast in the toaster oven then, when brown, fold in half. Serve with a cup of soup.

For a colorful assortment of garnishes, walk through the produce section of your grocery store and let your imagination run wild. Add sprouts to your favorite sandwich. Have you ever tried roasted bell peppers on a sandwich? Red or yellow bell peppers are especially delicious this way. Or use strips of roasted chile peppers for outstanding flavor. Try fresh spinach when you might normally use lettuce.

Why not try a combination of plain reduced-fat yogurt, reduced-fat mayonnaise, alfalfa sprouts, and finely chopped cucumber added to a sliced turkey breast on pumpernickel sandwich? Or use the same mixture with chopped water chestnuts instead of cucumber.

Blend a little lemon thyme in your reduced-fat mayonnaise then let it stand a couple of hours to blend the flavors. It's great with poultry or fish sandwiches.

As you browse through this book, look for ideas that appeal to you. For a light but special sandwich lunch, try Crabmeat Spread, page 35, served on fresh sourdough rolls with tomato slices and sprouts.

Chipped Turkey Sandwich

Barbecue sauce gives hearty flavor to this Super Bowl special.

2   pounds cooked
      turkey white meat, sliced
      very thin*

About 1 cup Grandma's
Barbecue Sauce, page 240

10   French bread-type buns
      or hard rolls

Preheat the oven to 350°F (175°C). Chop the turkey very fine. Place in a 2-quart shallow baking dish; pour desired amount of the sauce over the turkey. Cover and heat in the oven for about 30 minutes, or microwave just until heated. Spoon onto buns and serve.

Yield: 10 servings

Serving suggestions:

✦ Carrot sticks, celery, broccoli
   florets, with reduced-fat
   Ranch dressing

✦ Baked Corn Chips

✦ Lettuce

✦ Pickles, dill or sweet

✦ Pineapple Cookies, page 287

✦ Variety of fresh fruit

＊ This can also be purchased at your favorite deli.

1 serving contains: *Cal 538kc, Prot 40gm, Fat 5gm, Chol 76mg, Carb 81gm, Fib trace, Sodium 999mg*

Cheesy Chicken Sandwich

A delicious blending of flavors.

Pound the chicken breasts to flatten. Combine the salt, lemon pepper, and flour; dredge the chicken pieces in the flour mixture. Melt the margarine in a large nonstick skillet over medium-high heat. Add the chicken pieces and cook for 15 to 20 minutes or until brown and tender. Preheat the broiler. While the chicken is cooking, combine the mayonnaise, dill, green onion, and cheese in a small bowl. Lay the halved muffins on a clean surface. Spread half of the dressing mixture over the muffins, then top each muffin half with a piece of chicken. Set a pineapple ring on top of the chicken; spread the remaining dressing mixture over all. Broil for 3 to 4 minutes or until brown. Top with the remaining muffin halves and serve.

Yield: 6 servings

1 serving contains: *Cal 334kc, Prot 34gm, Fat 5gm, Chol 78mg, Carb 35gm, Fib trace, Sodium 566mg*

6	boneless, skinless chicken breast halves
1/4	teaspoon salt
1/8	teaspoon lemon pepper
2	tablespoons all-purpose flour
1	teaspoon margarine
1/4	cup reduced-fat mayonnaise
1/2	teaspoon dill weed
1/4	cup finely chopped green onion
1/3	cup shredded reduced-fat Cheddar cheese
6	English muffins, halved, toasted
6	pineapple rings, drained, fresh or canned

Serving suggestions:

✦ Macaroni Salad, page 105

✦ Best Oatmeal Cookies, page 280

Chicken Curry Sandwich

Use leftovers for a delicious supper.

4   slices whole wheat bread, toasted

8   slices cooked white chicken meat, about $^1/_3$ pound

4   thin slices cranberry sauce, about 3 ounces

$^1/_3$ cup reduced-fat mayonnaise

$^1/_4$ cup minced celery

$^1/_4$ cup minced onion

Dash of curry powder

Preheat the broiler. Place the toasted bread on a baking sheet; arrange 2 chicken slices on each piece. Lay the cranberry slices on top of the chicken. In a small bowl, combine mayonnaise, celery, and onion; spoon over the cranberries. Sprinkle the curry powder over all. Place under the broiler and heat until bubbling and slightly brown. Serve immediately.

Yield: 4 servings

1 serving contains: *Cal 183kc, Prot 14gm, Fat 5gm, Chol 29mg, Carb 23gm, Fib 3gm, Sodium 254mg*

Serving suggestions:

✦ Joyce's Cream of Broccoli Soup, page 58

✦ Sliced fresh fruit

Turkey Rollups

Have ingredients on hand for a quick meal.

Combine the mayonnaise and mustard, spread on tortillas; distribute the turkey, cheese, lettuce, tomatoes, and onion evenly between tortillas. Roll up jelly-roll fashion; if necessary use wooden picks to hold in place. Cut into thirds and serve i mmediately.

Yield: 4 servings

1 serving contains: *Cal 410kc, Prot 30gm, Fat 14gm, Chol 61mg, Carb 40gm, Fib 3gm, Sodium 1231mg*

1	tablespoon reduced-fat mayonnaise
1	teaspoon spicy brown mustard
4	(10-inch) flour tortillas
$1/2$	pound smoked turkey, sliced thin
4	very thin slices part-skim mozzarella cheese
1	cup chopped lettuce
1	tomato, chopped
$1/4$	thinly sliced sweet onion

Serving suggestions:

✦ **Macaroni Salad, page 105**

✦ **Fresh Fruit Kabobs, page 43**

Hot Puffy Chicken Sandwiches

You will like this unusual sandwich.

2   cups finely chopped cooked chicken white meat

$1/2$ cup finely chopped celery

$1/3$ cup reduced-fat mayonnaise

1   tablespoon lemon juice

6   slices whole wheat bread, toasted

3   egg whites

$1/2$ cup shredded reduced-fat Cheddar cheese

$1/8$ teaspoon dill weed

Preheat the broiler. In a medium-size bowl, combine the chicken, celery, mayonnaise, and lemon juice. Place the toasted bread on a baking sheet; spread the chicken mixture on the toast. In a large bowl, beat the egg whites until stiff peaks form; gently fold in the cheese and dill. Spread over the chicken. Broil for 8 to 10 minutes or until golden brown. Serve immediately.

Yield: 6 servings

1 serving contains: *Cal 218kc, Prot 25gm, Fat 7gm, Chol 57mg, Carb 16gm, Fib 3gm, Sodium 363mg*

Serving suggestions:

✦ Fresh Fruit Salad, page 91

✦ Gingerbread, page 274

Salmon Burgers

A different, exciting sandwich.

Prepare the Salmon Patties, making 6 patties. Cook as directed; set aside. Lay the sandwich buns on a clean surface. Spread the mustard on the bottom half of each bun and set a salmon patty on top. Garnish as desired and serve.

Yield: 6 servings

1 serving contains: *Cal 299kc, Prot 20gm, Fat 8gm, Chol 31mg, Carb 34gm, Fib 1gm, Sodium 752mg*

1	recipe Salmon Patties, page 176
6	soft whole wheat sandwich buns, halved
3	teaspoons brown mustard

Sweet onion slices, sprouts to garnish

Serving suggestions:

✦ Sliced tomatoes and cucumbers

✦ Joy's Pear-Crumble Pie, page 298

Sloppy Joes

New twist for an old favorite.

¹/₄ cup finely chopped onion

¹/₄ cup finely chopped green bell pepper

2 tablespoons water

1 pound ground turkey

1 cup Grandma's Barbecue Sauce, page 240

6 soft whole wheat sandwich buns

Crisp sweet pickles to garnish

In a large cast-iron skillet or heavy saucepan over low heat, cook the onion and green pepper in the water until tender. Add the ground turkey and cook, stirring often, until done and it has lost its pink color. Stir in the sauce. Simmer, uncovered, for about 30 minutes. Spoon onto the buns and serve with pickles.

Yield: 6 servings

1 serving contains: *Cal 381kc, Prot 14gm, Fat 4gm, Chol 32mg, Carb 28gm, Fib trace, Sodium 487mg*

Serving suggestions:

✦ Oven French Fries, page 219

✦ Applesauce Bars, page 267

Soupy Chicken Sandwiches

Great supper for a cold winter night.

Preheat the broiler. Heat the oil in a medium-size saucepan over medium-high heat. Add the green onion and sauté until wilted. Stir in the soup or sauce, milk, and dill. Add the chicken; stir gently until heated through. Place the toasted bread on a baking sheet; arrange the chicken mixture over the toast. Set a tomato slice on top of each sandwich, then a slice of cheese. Sprinkle with Parmesan cheese. Broil for 8 to 10 minutes or until lightly browned and bubbling.

Yield: 6 servings

1 serving contains: *Cal 290k, Prot 26gm, Fat 12gm, Chol 56mg, Carb 20gm, Fib 4gm, Sodium 884mg*

1	teaspoon extra-virgin olive oil
$1/2$	cup thinly sliced green onion
1	(10-ounce) can cream of mushroom soup, not diluted, or Basic White Sauce with mushrooms, page 242
$1/2$	cup skim milk
$1/4$	teaspoon dill weed
2	cups finely chopped cooked white chicken meat
6	slices whole wheat bread, toasted
6	slices tomato, about 4 ounces
6	slices reduced-fat Cheddar cheese, $4 1/2$ ounces
$1/4$	cup grated Parmesan cheese

Serving suggestions:

✦ Carrot sticks

✦ Baked corn chips

✦ Chocolate Pudding, page 305

Desserts

Fresh fruit is the greatest natural dessert. However, there are times when we crave something else. This section was compiled to use when the craving is overwhelming. These desserts are lower in calories, saturated fat, and cholesterol because they are made with polyunsaturated oils and margarines, and less of them, plus less sugar. I use skim milk and only egg white or egg substitutes; there's not much salt, either.

I have included some two-crust fruit pies, but I only make these on very special occasions. However, I do make basically the same recipe only using the bottom crust and then substitute a crumb topping in place of the top crust. This will greatly reduce the fat content. Refer to the example in Joy's Pear-Crumble Pie, page 298.

Desserts made with sugars should be prepared only for very special occasions. Angel food cake, fresh fruit, gelatin, sorbet, and ices are good alternatives to high-calorie desserts.

Grapefruit with Honey

Yummy, quick, and healthy.

1 grapefruit, cut in half
2 teaspoons honey
Fresh mint, chopped

Preheat the oven to broil. Place the grapefruit cut side up on a baking dish. Spoon the honey into the core, sprinkle with the mint, and broil lightly. Serve immediately.

Yield: 2 servings

Variations:

✦ Sprinkle with $\frac{1}{8}$ teaspoon ground cinnamon instead of mint.

✦ Sprinkle with 1 tablespoon oat bran before broiling.

1 serving contains: *Cal 59kc, Prot 1gm, Fat trace, Chol 0, Carb 15gm, Fib 2gm, Sodium trace*

Cantaloupe Bowls

A refreshingly fresh dessert.

Cut the cantaloupe in half and remove seeds. Cut the edges in a sawtooth design. Using a melon baller, remove the melon flesh and place in a medium-size bowl. Add the strawberries, kiwi, and mint leaves. Toss gently, then spoon into the cantaloupe shells. Serve immediately.

Yield: 14 (^{1}/2-cup) servings

1 serving contains: *Cal 36kc, Prot 1gm, Fat trace, Chol 0, Carb 8gm, Fib 2gm, Sodium 5mg*

1	large ripe cantaloupe
2	pints fresh strawberries, washed, hulled
2	kiwifruit, sliced
Fresh spearmint leaves	

Dutch Apple Cake

Serve warm with Vanilla Sauce, page 250.

1	cup unbleached or all-purpose flour, sifted
5	tablespoons sugar, divided
1	teaspoon baking powder
2	tablespoons margarine, divided
2	egg whites, slightly beaten
$\frac{1}{4}$	cup skim milk
$\frac{1}{2}$	teaspoon vanilla extract
4	cups sliced, peeled apples
1	teaspoon ground cinnamon

Preheat the oven to 375°F (190°C). Grease and flour a 9-inch tart or pie pan. In a mixing bowl, combine the flour, 2 tablespoons sugar, and baking powder. With a pastry blender or 2 knives, cut in 1½ tablespoons of the margarine. Add the egg whites, milk, and vanilla; beat until smooth. The batter will be stiff. Spoon into the prepared pan and spread the batter to fit pan. Arrange the apple slices, overlapping, in 2 concentric circles to cover batter. In a small bowl, combine 3 tablespoons sugar and cinnamon; sprinkle over the apple slices. Dot with the remaining margarine. Bake for 30 minutes. Cool for 10 minutes before serving.

Yield: 6 servings

1 serving contains: *Cal 183kc, Prot 4gm, Fat 2gm, Chol trace, Carb 38gm, Fib 2gm, Sodium 125mg*

Applesauce Bars

A moist, cinnamony treat.

Preheat the oven to 350°F (175°C). Lightly grease and flour a 13 x 9-inch baking pan. Sift the flour, baking soda, and spices into a medium-size bowl; set aside. In a large mixing bowl, beat the margarine, brown sugar, and granulated sugar until light and fluffy. Stir in the egg whites and applesauce. Gradually add the flour mixture, beating well after each addition. Fold in the raisins. Pour into prepared pan. Bake for 25 to 30 minutes or until a wooden pick comes out clean. Let cool until slightly warm; prepare icing.

For the icing: In a medium-size bowl, mix the powdered sugar, milk, and vanilla; beat until smooth. Drizzle over the warm cake. Cool completely before cutting into bars.

Yield: 12 servings

1 serving with icing contains: *Cal 256kc, Prot 3gm, Fat 4gm, Chol trace, Carb 53gm, Fib 2gm, Sodium 176mg*

2	cups unbleached or all-purpose flour
1	teaspoon baking soda
1	teaspoon ground cinnamon
1	teaspoon ground nutmeg
1/2	teaspoon ground cloves
1/2	cup margarine, room temperature
1/2	cup firmly packed brown sugar
1/2	cup granulated sugar
2	egg whites, slightly beaten
1	cup unsweetened applesauce
1	cup raisins

Icing:

1	cup sifted powdered sugar
2	tablespoons warm skim milk
1/2	teaspoon vanilla extract

Banana Cake

Make a day ahead for a truly moist banana flavor.

For special occasions, top with 7-Minute Frosting, page 279.

$2^1/_2$	cups cake flour
$1^2/_3$	cups sugar
$1^1/_4$	teaspoons baking powder
$1^1/_4$	teaspoons baking soda
$1/_3$	cup margarine, room temperature
$1/_3$	cup canola oil
$1^1/_4$	cups mashed bananas, very ripe
$2/_3$	cup sour skim milk, divided
4	egg whites, slightly beaten

Preheat the oven to 350°F (175°C). Grease and flour two 9-inch cake pans or one 13 x 9-inch baking pan. Sift the flour, sugar, baking powder, and baking soda together into a large mixing bowl. Add the margarine, oil, bananas, and half the milk; beat at medium speed for 2 minutes. Add the egg whites and the remaining milk; beat for 2 minutes longer. Pour into the prepared pans. Bake the 9-inch layers for 35 minutes or the 13 x 9-inch pan for 45 to 50 minutes, or until a wooden pick comes out clean. Invert onto a cooling rack. Let stand for 10 minutes before removing from the pan. Cool completely before serving.

Yield: 12 servings

1 serving without frosting contains: *Cal 296kc, Prot 4gm, Fat 9gm, Chol trace, Carb 52gm, Fib 1gm, Sodium 206mg*

Blueberry Tea Cake

Perfect dessert for brunch.

Preheat the oven to 375°F (190°C). Grease and flour a 9-inch square baking pan. In a large mixing bowl, beat together the margarine and sugar until light and fluffy. Add the egg whites and milk; blend well. Sift together the flour and baking soda into a medium-size bowl. Stir into the margarine mixture. Fold in the blueberries. Spoon into the prepared pan.

For the topping: Combine the sugar, flour, cinnamon, nutmeg, and allspice into a small bowl. Cut in the margarine with a pastry blender. Sprinkle over the cake batter.

Bake for 40 to 45 minutes or until a wooden pick comes out clean. Serve warm or cooled.

Yield: 9 servings

1 serving contains: *Cal 276kc, Prot 5gm, Fat 4gm, Chol trace, Carb 56gm, Fib 2gm, Sodium 189mg*

1/4 cup margarine, room temperature

3/4 cup sugar

2 egg whites, slightly beaten

1/2 cup skim milk

2 cups unbleached or all-purpose flour

2 teaspoons baking powder

2 cups fresh or frozen blueberries

Topping:

1/2 cup sugar

1/4 cup all-purpose flour

1/2 teaspoon ground cinnamon

1/2 teaspoon ground nutmeg

1/4 teaspoon ground allspice

2 tablespoons margarine, room temperature

Caroline's Chocolate Cake

If you like chocolate cake, this will be your favorite.

$1/2$	cup margarine, room temperature
$1^3/4$	cups sugar, divided
$1^2/3$	cups cold water, divided
$1/2$	cup cocoa
1	teaspoon vanilla extract
$2^1/2$	cups sifted cake flour
3	egg whites
$1^1/2$	teaspoons baking soda

Preheat the oven to 350°F (175°C). Grease and flour two (9-inch square) or one (13 x 9-inch) baking pan. In a large mixing bowl, beat margarine and 1 cup sugar until light and fluffy. Add $1/3$ cup cold water, cocoa, and vanilla, mixing well. Add the flour alternately with 1 cup water, beating after each addition. In a mixing bowl, beat egg whites lightly; gradually add $3/4$ cup sugar. Beat until stiff peaks form. Fold beaten egg whites into batter. Dissolve soda in remaining $1/3$ cup water, stir into batter. Pour batter into prepared pans. Bake 9-inch layers for 30 to 35 minutes, 13 x 9-inch pan for 35 to 40 minutes, or until a wooden pick comes out clean. Invert onto cooling racks. Let stand 10 minutes before removing pan. Cool completely before frosting and serving.

Yield: 12 servings

Note: Use 7-Minute Frosting, page 279, if desired.

1 serving without frosting contains: *Cal 242kc, Prot 4gm, Fat 5gm, Chol 0, Carb 45gm, Fib 1gm, Sodium 208mg*

Johnny's Oatmeal Cake

So moist and yummy.

Preheat the oven to 350°F (175°C). Grease and flour a 9-inch square baking pan. Place the oats in a medium-size bowl. Pour the boiling water over the oats; cover and let stand for 20 minutes. In a large mixing bowl, beat the margarine and sugars until light and fluffy. Blend in the vanilla and egg whites. Add the oats mixture and mix well. Sift together the flour, baking soda, cinnamon, and nutmeg into a medium-size bowl. Add to the oats mixture. Add the raisins and mix well. Pour the batter into the prepared pan. Bake for 50 to 55 minutes. Cool completely before frosting and serving.

For the frosting: Combine the margarine, sugars, and milk in a small saucepan. Bring to a boil and boil 1 minute. Stir in the vanilla and spoon over the cooled cake.

Yield: 9 servings

1 serving with frosting contains: *Cal 373kc, Prot 5gm, Fat 7gm, Chol 0, Carb 76gm, Fib 2gm, Sodium 257mg*

1	cup old-fashioned rolled oats, uncooked
1¼	cups boiling water
½	cup margarine, room temperature
1	cup granulated sugar
1	cup firmly packed brown sugar
1	teaspoon vanilla extract
3	egg whites, slightly beaten
1½	cups unbleached or all-purpose flour
1	teaspoon baking soda
¾	teaspoon ground cinnamon
¼	teaspoon ground nutmeg
½	cup raisins

Frosting:

1	tablespoon margarine, melted
1	tablespoon brown sugar
1	tablespoon granulated sugar
1	tablespoon skim milk
½	teaspoon vanilla extract

Sewing-Circle Favorite Apple Cake

Apple pieces and raisins give this cake a delightful texture.

1³/₄	cups sugar
³/₄	cup canola oil
4	egg whites, slightly beaten
2	cups unbleached or all-purpose flour
1	teaspoon baking soda
1	tablespoon ground cinnamon
¹/₈	teaspoon ground cloves
1	teaspoon ground nutmeg
5	large apples, peeled, cut into bite-size pieces (5 to 6 cups)
1	cup raisins
2	tablespoons powdered sugar

Preheat the oven to 350°F (175°C). Lightly spray a 13 x 9-inch baking pan with vegetable spray. In a large bowl, combine the sugar and oil; stir in the egg whites. Add the flour, baking soda, cinnamon, cloves, and nutmeg; mix well. Fold in the apples and raisins. Spoon into the prepared pan; the batter will be thick. Bake for 50 to 55 minutes or until a wooden pick comes out clean. Sift the powdered sugar over the cake while still warm. Cool before serving.

Yield: 12 servings

1 serving contains: *Cal 378kc, Prot 4gm, Fat 14gm, Chol 0, Carb 63gm, Fib 3gm, Sodium 88mg*

Strawberry Shortcake

A delightful springtime dessert.

Preheat the oven to 350°F (175°C). Lightly grease and flour an 8-inch square baking pan. In a medium-size mixing bowl, combine the Baking Mix, sugar, egg whites, water, and vanilla; beat at low speed until moistened. Beat at medium speed for 4 minutes, scraping the sides of the bowl occasionally. Pour into the prepared pan. Bake for 30 minutes or until a wooden pick comes out clean. Cool. While the cake is baking, slice the strawberries and sprinkle with sugar. Chill until ready to use. To serve, cut a square of cake, place in dessert dish and top with strawberries.

Yield: 9 servings

1 serving contains: *Cal 194kc, Prot 3gm, Fat 3gm, Chol trace, Carb 40gm, Fib 3gm, Sodium 190mg*

1 1/2	cups Baking Mix, page 66
1/2	cup sugar
2	egg whites, slightly beaten
1/2	cup water
1	teaspoon vanilla extract
2	quarts strawberries, hulled, rinsed
1/2	cup sugar or artificial sweetener to taste

273

Gingerbread

Moist, spicy, and delicious; top it with Lemon-Raisin Sauce, page 251.

$1/2$ cup canola oil

2   tablespoons brown sugar

2   egg whites, slightly beaten

1   cup dark molasses

1   cup boiling water

$2^1/4$ cups unbleached or all-purpose flour

1   teaspoon baking soda

1   teaspoon ground ginger

1   teaspoon ground cinnamon

$1/8$ teaspoon ground allspice

Preheat the oven to 350°F (175°C). Lightly grease and flour an 8-inch square baking pan. In a large bowl, combine the oil, sugar, and egg whites. Stir in the molasses and water. Sift together the flour, baking soda, ginger, cinnamon, and allspice into a medium-size bowl. Stir into the molasses mixture. Pour into the prepared pan. Bake for 45 to 50 minutes. Cool before serving.

Yield: 9 servings

1 serving contains: *Cal 317kc, Prot 4gm, Fat 12gm, Chol 0, Carb 47gm, Fib 1gm, Sodium 136mg*

Pineapple-Cherry Upside-Down Cake

One of my childhood favorites.

Preheat the oven to 350°F (175°C). In a round or square 8-inch baking pan, melt the margarine; sprinkle with brown sugar. Arrange the pineapple slices evenly around the pan, then place a cherry in the center of each slice. In a large mixing bowl, combine the flour and sugar. Blend in the oil and ¼ cup of the milk; beat for 2 minutes. Stir in the baking powder, remaining milk, egg whites, and vanilla; beat at medium speed for 2 minutes longer. Pour the batter over the pineapple. Bake for 35 to 40 minutes or until a wooden pick comes out clean. Immediately invert onto a serving plate; leave the pan over the cake for about 5 minutes, then remove. Serve warm or cooled.

Yield: 8 servings

1 serving contains: *Cal 284kc, Prot 3gm, Fat 9gm, Chol trace, Carb 50gm, Fib 1gm, Sodium 130mg*

2	tablespoons margarine
½	cup firmly packed brown sugar
6	canned pineapple slices
6	maraschino cherries
1	cup cake flour, sifted
¾	cup sugar
¼	cup canola oil
½	cup skim milk, divided
1½	teaspoons baking powder
3	egg whites, slightly beaten
½	teaspoon vanilla extract

Lemon Bundt Cake

Our family loves this cake—they always come back for more.

1 (18.5-ounce) box white cake mix

1 (3.4-ounce) package instant lemon pudding

Juice of 2 fresh lemons, divided

Zest from 2 fresh lemons, divided

3/4 cup egg substitute*

4 egg whites*

1 cup plain reduced-fat yogurt

1/2 cup applesauce

1/2 cup water

2 cups sifted powdered sugar

2 teaspoons margarine, melted

1 tablespoon skim milk

Preheat the oven to 350°F (175°C). Spray a Bundt pan or angel food pan with vegetable spray.

Combine the cake mix, pudding, juice from 1 lemon, egg substitute, egg whites, yogurt, applesauce, and water in a large mixing bowl; beat on medium speed for 2 minutes. Stir in the zest from 1 lemon. Pour the batter into the prepared Bundt pan; bake for 50 to 55 minutes or until a wooden pick comes out clean. Cool in the pan on a wire rack for 15 minutes; remove from the pan and cool completely. When cool; combine the powdered sugar, margarine, milk, and remaining lemon juice in a medium mixing bowl; the mixture should be fairly thin. Drizzle over the top of the cake letting it run down the sides. Sprinkle the remaining zest over the moist glaze.

Yield: 14 servings

⁎ You can substitute 1 cup of whole eggs (about 4) in place of egg substitute and egg white, but it will add a significant amount of fat, cholesterol and calories.

1 serving contains: *Cal 294kc, Prot 5gm, Fat 6gm, Chol 1mg, Carb 57gm, Fib trace, Sodium 296mg*

Butterscotch Apples

A favorite fall dessert when the apples are fresh from the orchard.

Preheat the oven to 375°F (190°C). Spray an 8 or 9-inch round baking dish with vegetable spray. Arrange the apples in the prepared dish. Combine the brown sugar, cinnamon, nutmeg, and flour in small bowl; blend well. Sprinkle evenly over the apples. Pour the orange juice over the apples.

For the topping, combine the brown sugar and flour in a small bowl; stir. Cut in the margarine with a pastry blender until the mixture resembles coarse meal. Spread over the apples and bake, covered, for 20 minutes. Uncover and continue baking until lightly browned and tender.

Yield: 4 servings

1 serving contains: *Cal 500kc, Prot 3gm, Fat 12gm, Chol 0, Carb 102gm, Fib 5gm, Sodium 156mg*

6	large tart apples, peeled and sliced
$1^1/2$	cup packed brown sugar
$1^1/2$	teaspoon cinnamon
$^1/4$	teaspoon nutmeg
2	tablespoons flour
$^1/4$	cup orange juice

Topping:

$^1/2$	cup brown sugar
$^1/3$	cup flour
$^1/4$	cup margarine

Springfield Frosting

A light and creamy frosting.

2½ tablespoons all-purpose flour

½ cup skim milk

½ cup margarine

½ cup powdered sugar

1 teaspoon vanilla extract

In a small saucepan, blend the flour and milk together; stir over medium heat until thickened. Set aside to cool. In a mixer, beat the margarine and powdered sugar until creamy. Add the vanilla; then the milk mixture. Beat until creamy and smooth. Use to frost the cake of your choice. The frosting may be stored several days in the refrigerator.

Yield: 12 servings; will frost a 13 x 9-inch cake

1 serving contains: *Cal 59kc, Prot 1gm, Fat 4gm, Chol trace, Carb 6gm, Fib trace, Sodium 98mg*

7-Minute Frosting

An easy, reliable frosting.

In the bottom of a double boiler, bring about 1 cup of water to a boil. In the top of the double boiler, combine the egg whites, sugar, cream of tartar, syrup, and water. Set the top pan over the boiling water on medium heat. Beat the mixture with an electric mixer on high speed until it holds a stiff peak. Add the vanilla and blend. Use to frost cooled cake of your choice.

Yield: 12 servings, will frost a 13 x 9-inch cake

1 serving contains: *Cal 83kc, Prot 1gm, Fat 0, Chol 0, Carb 21gm, Fib 0, Sodium 10mg*

2	egg whites
1 $^1/_4$	cups sugar
$^1/_2$	teaspoon cream of tartar
1	tablespoon light corn syrup
$^1/_3$	cup water
1 $^1/_2$	teaspoons vanilla extract

Best Oatmeal Cookies

The name says it all.

3/4 cup margarine,
     room temperature

1   cup granulated sugar

1/2 cup firmly packed brown
     sugar

2   egg whites,
     slightly beaten

1 1/2 cups unbleached
     or all-purpose flour

1   teaspoon baking soda

1   teaspoon ground
     cinnamon

1/4 teaspoon ground
     nutmeg

1 1/2 cups oats, uncooked

1   cup raisins

1   teaspoon vanilla
     extract

In a large mixing bowl, beat the margarine and sugars until light and fluffy. Add the egg whites. In a medium-size bowl, combine flour, baking soda, cinnamon, and nutmeg; add to the sugar mixture. Stir in the oats, raisins, and vanilla. Chill for 1 hour. Preheat the oven to 350°F (175°C). Roll a teaspoon of dough into a ball and place on an ungreased cookie sheet. Grease the bottom of a glass with margarine, dip the glass in sugar, and use to flatten the ball of dough. Continue until the cookie sheet is full, leaving adequate space between cookies. Bake for 10 minutes. Cool on wire racks.

Yield: About 55 cookies

1 cookie contains: *Cal 61kc, Prot 1gm, Fat 1gm, Chol 0, Carb 12gm, Fib trace, Sodium 48mg*

Date Pinwheels

Freeze the cookie dough rolls so you can slice and bake as needed.

For the filling: In a medium-size saucepan, combine the dates, water, and sugar. Bring to a boil and simmer for 5 minutes, stirring often. Set aside to cool.

For the dough: In a large mixing bowl, beat the margarine, brown sugar, and granulated sugar until light and fluffy. Add the vanilla and egg whites; mix well. In a medium-size bowl, combine the flour and baking soda; add to the creamed mixture and mix well. Refrigerate until the dough is firm enough to roll. Cut the dough in half. On a floured surface, roll each half into a 12 x 9-inch rectangle; spread with the filling. Roll up tightly, jelly-roll fashion. Cover with foil or plastic wrap. Refrigerate overnight or freeze.

To bake, preheat the oven to 375°F (190°C). Lightly spray a cookie sheet with vegetable spray. Cut the chilled dough into $1/8$-inch-thick slices; place on the prepared cookie sheet. Bake for 10 minutes. Cool on wire racks.

Yield: 50 pinwheels

1 pinwheel contains: *Cal 54kc, Prot 1gm, Fat 1gm, Chol 0, Carb 12gm, Fib trace, Sodium 22mg*

Filling:
1   (7 $1/4$-ounce) package dates, chopped
$1/3$ cup water
$1/4$ cup sugar

Dough:
$1/3$ cup margarine or butter, room temperature
$1/2$ cup firmly packed brown sugar
$1/2$ cup granulated sugar
$1/2$ teaspoon vanilla extract
2   egg whites, slightly beaten
2   cups unbleached or all-purpose flour
$1/4$ teaspoon baking soda

English Teacakes

A nice little dessert, yet not too sweet.

$1/2$	cup margarine or butter, room temperature
1	cup sugar, divided
3	egg whites, slightly beaten, divided
$1^3/4$	cups all-purpose flour
$1^1/2$	teaspoons baking powder
3	tablespoons skim milk
$1/2$	cup chopped candied fruit
$1/2$	cup raisins

In a large mixing bowl, beat the margarine, $3/4$ cup sugar, and 2 egg whites until smooth. In a medium-size bowl combine the flour and baking powder. Add the milk and flour to the sugar mixture alternately, mixing well after each addition. Stir in the candied fruit and raisins; mix well. Refrigerate for at least 1 hour. Preheat the oven to 400°F (205°C). Lightly spray a cookie sheet with vegetable spray. Place the remaining $1/4$ cup sugar in a shallow bowl. Roll the dough into walnut-size balls, dip the top of each ball into the remaining egg white, then into the sugar. Bake for 12 to 15 minutes or until golden brown. Cool on wire racks.

Yield: 55 cakes

1 cookie contains: *Cal 45kc, Prot 1gm, Fat 1gm, Chol trace, Carb 9gm, Fib trace, Sodium 34mg*

Betty's Apple Cookies

Wonderfully moist and flavorful.

Preheat the oven to 350°F (175°C). Lightly spray a cookie sheet with vegetable spray. In a medium bowl, mix the flour, baking soda, cloves, cinnamon, and nutmeg. In a large mixing bowl, beat the margarine and sugar until light and fluffy. Add the egg whites, then juice or water, stirring to mix well. Gradually add the dry ingredients; fold in the apples and raisins. Drop by teaspoonfuls onto the prepared cookie sheet. Bake for 12 to 15 minutes. Cool on wire racks.

Yield: 60 cookies

1 cookie contains: *Cal 50kc, Prot 1gm, Fat 1gm, Chol 0, Carb 10gm, Fib trace, Sodium 36mg*

2	cups unbleached or all-purpose flour
1	teaspoon baking soda
1	teaspoon ground cloves
$1/2$	teaspoon ground cinnamon
$1/2$	teaspoon ground nutmeg
$1/2$	cup margarine or butter, room temperature
$1^1/3$	cups firmly packed brown sugar
2	egg whites, slightly beaten
$1/4$	cup apple juice or water
1	cup finely chopped apples
1	cup raisins

Grandma's Orange Cookies

Smooth texture and orange flavor bring back special memories.

4 1/2 cups unbleached or all-purpose flour

1 teaspoon baking soda

2 teaspoons baking powder

3/4 cup margarine or butter, room temperature

2 cups sugar

4 egg whites, slightly beaten

1/2 cup orange juice

1 tablespoon grated orange peel

3/4 cup sour skim milk

Orange Cookie Icing, page 289

Preheat the oven to 350°F (175°C). Lightly spray a cookie sheet with vegetable spray. In a medium bowl mix the flour, baking soda, and baking powder. In a large mixing bowl, beat the margarine and sugar until light and fluffy. Add the egg whites, juice, and orange peel. Gradually add the flour mixture, alternating with the sour milk; mix thoroughly. Drop by teaspoonfuls onto the prepared cookie sheet. Bake for 8 minutes or until set. Cool on wire racks. Ice if desired.

Yield: About 90 cookies

1 cookie without icing contains: *Cal 48kc, Prot 1gm, Fat 1gm, Chol trace, Carb 9gm, Fib trace, Sodium 39mg*

1 cookie with icing contains: *Cal 57kc, Prot 1gm, Fat 1gm, Chol trace, Carb 11gm, Fib trace, Sodium 40mg*

Holiday Fruit Cookies

So easy to make, and they freeze well, too.

Preheat the oven to 400°F (205°C). Lightly spray a cookie sheet with vegetable spray. In a large mixing bowl, beat the margarine, sugar, and egg whites. Stir in the sour milk. Gradually add the flour and baking soda; mix well. Fold in the fruit. Drop by teaspoonfuls onto the prepared cookie sheet. Bake for 8 to 10 minutes or until set. Cool on wire racks.

Yield: 85 cookies

1 cookie contains: *Cal 73kc, Prot 1gm, Fat 1gm, Chol trace, Carb 16gm, Fib 1gm, Sodium 44mg*

1	cup margarine or butter, room temperature
2	cups firmly packed brown sugar
3	egg whites, slightly beaten
$1/2$	cup sour skim milk
$3^1/2$	cups unbleached or all-purpose flour
1	teaspoon baking soda
2	cups chopped candied fruit
2	cups chopped dates

Orange Granola Cookies

So yummy and nutritious.

1/2 cup margarine or butter, room temperature

1/2 cup sugar

2 egg whites, slightly beaten

1/2 cup honey

1/3 cup frozen orange juice concentrate

2 1/4 cups unbleached or all-purpose flour

2 1/2 teaspoons baking powder

1/2 teaspoon baking soda

2 teaspoons ground cinnamon

1/4 teaspoon ground cloves

1 cup oats, uncooked

1 cup raisins

Preheat the oven to 350°F (175°C). Lightly spray a cookie sheet with vegetable spray. In a large mixing bowl, beat the margarine and sugar until light and fluffy. Beat in the egg whites. Combine the honey and orange juice in a small bowl; set aside. In a medium-size bowl, combine the flour, baking powder, baking soda, cinnamon, and cloves. Gradually add the flour mixture to the margarine mixture, alternating with the honey mixture. Stir in the oats and raisins. Drop by teaspoonfuls onto the prepared cookie sheet. Bake for about 12 minutes or until firm to the touch. Cool on wire racks.

Yield: 50 cookies

1 cookie contains: *Cal 65kc, Prot 1gm, Fat 1gm, Chol 0, Carb 13gm, Fib trace, Sodium 50mg*

Pineapple Cookies

Moist texture and tangy flavor.

Preheat the oven to 350°F (175°C). Lightly spray a cookie sheet with vegetable spray. In a large mixing bowl, beat the margarine and sugar until light and fluffy. Add the egg whites and beat well. Stir in the pineapple and vanilla. In a medium-size bowl, combine the flour, baking powder, and baking soda. Gradually add the flour mixture to the creamed mixture, beating until smooth after each addition. Drop by teaspoonfuls onto the prepared cookie sheet. Bake for 10 minutes or until done. Cool on wire racks. Ice if desired.

Yield: 50 cookies

1 cookie without icing contains: *Cal 52kc, Prot 1gm, Fat 1gm, Chol 0, Carb 9gm, Fib trace, Sodium 48mg*

1 cookie with icing contains: *Cal 62kc, Prot 1gm, Fat 1gm, Chol trace, Carb 11gm, Fib trace, Sodium 49mg*

$2/3$ cup margarine or butter, room temperature

$1^1/4$ cups firmly packed brown sugar

3 egg whites, slightly beaten

$3/4$ cup crushed pineapple, well drained

1 teaspoon vanilla extract

2 cups unbleached or all-purpose flour

$1^1/2$ teaspoons baking powder

$1/4$ teaspoon baking soda

Vanilla Cookie Icing, page 290, optional

Pumpkin Cookies

Great flavor combination!

2 cups unbleached or all-purpose flour

1 teaspoon baking soda

1 teaspoon baking powder

1/8 teaspoon ground cloves

1 teaspoon ground cinnamon

1 cup sugar

3/4 cup margarine or butter, room temperature

2 egg whites, slightly beaten

1 cup cooked pumpkin, mashed

1 teaspoon vanilla extract

1 cup chopped dates

Brown Sugar Cookie Icing, page 291

Preheat the oven to 350°F (175°C). Lightly spray a cookie sheet with vegetable spray. In a medium-size bowl, combine the flour, baking soda, baking powder, cloves, and cinnamon. In a large mixing bowl, beat the sugar and margarine until light and fluffy. Add the egg whites, pumpkin, and vanilla. Gradually stir in the flour mixture; mix well. Fold in the dates. Drop by teaspoonfuls onto the prepared cookie sheet. Bake for 10 to 12 minutes. Cool on wire racks before icing.

Yield: 60 cookies

1 cookie without icing contains: *Cal 47kc, Prot 1gm, Fat 1gm, Chol 0, Carb 9gm, Fib trace, Sodium 49mg*

1 cookie with icing contains: *Cal 61kc, Prot 1gm, Fat 1gm, Chol trace, Carb 12gm, Fib trace, Sodium 52mg*

Orange Cookie Icing

Refreshing light flavor complements most cookies.

In a small bowl, mix the sugar, margarine, orange flavoring, milk, and peel; beat until smooth. Spread icing on each cookie; let set until firm.

Yield: Icing for 90 cookies

1 serving contains: *Cal 9kc, Prot trace, Fat trace, Chol trace, Carb 2gm, Fib 0, Sodium 1mg*

2	cups powdered sugar
1	teaspoon margarine or butter, room temperature
$1/2$	teaspoon orange flavoring
3	tablespoons skim milk
1	tablespoon grated orange peel

Vanilla Cookie Icing

Enhances a variety of cookies.

1½   cups powdered sugar

1   teaspoon margarine
      or butter,
      room temperature

½   teaspoon vanilla

2½   tablespoons skim milk

In a small bowl combine the sugar, margarine, vanilla, and milk; beat until smooth. Spread icing over each cookie.

Yield: Icing for 60 cookies

1 cookie contains: *Cal 10kc, Prot trace, Fat trace, Chol trace, Carb 2gm, Fib 0, Sodium 1mg*

Brown Sugar Cookie Icing

A nice change in taste.

In a medium-size saucepan combine the margarine, milk, and brown sugar; boil for 2 minutes. Remove from the heat and stir in the powdered sugar and vanilla; beat until smooth. Add more powdered sugar or milk if needed to make it spreading consistency. Spread icing over each cookie.

Yield: Icing for 60 cookies

1 serving contains: *Cal 21kc, Prot trace, Fat trace, Chol trace, Carb 5gm, Fib 0, Sodium 3mg*

1	tablespoon margarine or butter, room temperature
1/4	cup skim milk
1/2	cup firmly packed brown sugar
2	cups powdered sugar, sifted
1	teaspoon vanilla extract

Apples and Cranberries

A favorite dessert for fall!

4 cups chopped, peeled apples

3 cups cranberries, washed, drained

1½ cups granulated sugar

½ cup firmly packed brown sugar

1½ cups oats, uncooked

⅓ cup unbleached or all-purpose flour

½ teaspoon ground cinnamon

¼ teaspoon ground cloves

½ cup margarine or butter, melted

Preheat the oven to 350°F (175°C). In a large bowl, combine the apples, cranberries, and granulated sugar. Spread in a shallow 2-quart casserole or a 10-inch square pan. In a medium-size bowl, blend the brown sugar, oats, flour, and spices. Pour the melted margarine over the oatmeal mixture; blend well. Spread the topping over fruit. Bake, uncovered, for 1 hour. Serve warm.

Yield: 10 servings

Variation:

✦ Add ⅓ cup chopped pecans with the crumb topping if your diet permits.

1 serving contains: *Cal 291kc, Prot 2gm, Fat 6gm, Chol 0, Carb 61gm, Fib 1gm, Sodium 115mg*

Blueberry and Peach Crisp

Nice dessert for a patio meal. Nectarines can be substituted for peaches.

Preheat the oven to 350°F (175°C). Place the peach slices in a 9-inch pie plate; top with the blueberries. In a small bowl, blend the flour, sugar, and margarine with a pastry blender until crumbly; sprinkle over the fruit. Bake, uncovered, for 30 minutes or until bubbling and brown. Serve warm.

Yield: 6 servings

1 serving contains: *Cal 143kc, Prot 1gm, Fat 1gm, Chol 0, Carb 33gm, Fib 2gm, Sodium 30mg*

2	medium peaches, peeled, sliced, about $1^1/4$ cups
1	cup fresh or frozen blueberries
$1/2$	cup unbleached or all-purpose flour
$1/2$	cup firmly packed brown sugar
1	tablespoon margarine or butter, at room temperature

Cherry Cobbler

Cinnamon enhances the cherry flavor.

2	(21-ounce) cans cherry pie filling
$1/2$	teaspoon ground cinnamon
1	cup unbleached or all-purpose flour
1	tablespoon sugar
1	teaspoon baking powder

Pinch of ground ginger

$1/2$	cup skim milk
$3^1/2$	tablespoons canola oil

Preheat the oven to 400°F (205°C). Spoon the pie filling into a shallow 2-quart baking dish; sprinkle with the cinnamon. In a small bowl, combine the flour, sugar, baking powder, ginger, milk, and oil. Drop by teaspoonfuls onto the pie filling. Bake, uncovered, for 30 minutes or until nicely browned. Serve warm.

Yield: 12 servings

1 serving contains: *Cal 211kc, Prot 2gm, Fat 4gm, Chol trace, Carb 44gm, Fib 1gm, Sodium 41mg*

Grandma's Fruit Rings

Fresh peaches or apples are best in this old family favorite.

Preheat the oven to 350°F (175°C). In a small saucepan, combine the sugar and 1½ cups water; heat until the sugar dissolves. Pour into a shallow 10-inch square baking dish. In a large bowl, combine the Baking Mix and ⅔ cup water; stir until a soft dough forms. Turn out onto a floured pastry sheet and roll into a 12-inch square. Scatter the fruit over the dough; sprinkle with the cinnamon. Roll up dough jelly-roll style. Using a sharp knife, cut into 10 slices. Lay cut side up in the pan with the syrup. Bake for 45 minutes. Serve warm.

Yield: 10 servings

* You can substitute reduced-fat Bisquick; if using Bisquick, substitute skim milk for water.

1 serving with apples contains: *Cal 211kc, Prot 2gm, Fat 2gm, Chol trace, Carb 47gm, Fib 1gm, Sodium 229mg*

1½ cups sugar

1½ cups plus ⅔ cup water, divided

2¼ cups Baking Mix*, page 66

2½ cups finely chopped, peeled fruit

½ teaspoon ground cinnamon

295

Peach Torte

Delicious with hot tea.

1¼ cups plus 1 tablespoon unbleached or all-purpose flour, divided

¾ cup sugar, divided

¼ teaspoon baking powder

1 egg white, slightly beaten

¼ cup plus 1 tablespoon margarine or butter, room temperature, divided

2 tablespoons skim milk

4 large peaches, peeled, sliced, about 3 cups

¾ teaspoon ground cinnamon

Preheat the oven to 400°F (205°C). In a large bowl, combine 1¼ cups flour, ¼ cup sugar, and baking powder. Add the egg white, ¼ cup margarine, and milk; mix well. Spoon into a 9-inch cake pan, pressing around bottom and edges. Arrange peach slices on top of crust. In a small bowl, combine the remaining 1 tablespoon flour, ½ cup sugar, and the cinnamon. Sprinkle over the fruit. Dot with the remaining 1 tablespoon margarine. Bake for 15 minutes; reduce the heat to 350°F (175°C) and bake for 30 minutes longer. Serve warm or cooled.

Yield: 8 servings

1 serving contains: *Cal 196kc, Prot 3gm, Fat 4gm, Chol trace, Carb 39gm, Fib 2gm, Sodium 106mg*

Baked Pears and Raisins

New twist for an old standby. Top with whipped topping or reduced-fat ice milk.

Preheat the oven to 350°F (175°C). In a small bowl, combine the breadcrumbs, oat bran, sugar, cinnamon, and nutmeg; set aside. In a small mixing bowl, beat the egg white. Dip the pear halves in the beaten egg white, then in the breadcrumb mixture. Arrange the pears in a 10-inch square baking pan. Spoon the raisins into the cavities of the pears. Pour the water gently into the pan. Bake, uncovered, for 40 minutes or until tender. Serve warm.

Yield: 8 servings

1 serving contains: *Cal 148kc, Prot 3gm, Fat 1gm, Chol 0, Carb 35gm, Fib 4gm, Sodium 57mg*

$1/2$ cup fresh breadcrumbs

$1/4$ cup oat bran

$1/3$ cup firmly packed brown sugar

$1/4$ teaspoon ground cinnamon

$1/8$ teaspoon ground nutmeg

1 egg white

4 firm pears, peeled, cut in half, cored

$1/2$ cup raisins

$1/4$ cup water

Joy's Pear Crumble Pie

Pears and lemon peel give a nice smooth flavor.

6   medium pears, peeled, sliced, 6 to 7 cups

3   tablespoons lemon juice

$1/3$ cup sugar

2   tablespoons unbleached or all-purpose flour

$1/8$ teaspoon ground cinnamon

1   teaspoon grated lemon peel

1   (9-inch) unbaked pastry shell, page 302

Topping:

$1/2$ cup unbleached or all-purpose flour

$1/2$ cup sugar

$1/2$ teaspoon ground ginger

$1/2$ teaspoon ground cinnamon

$1/4$ cup margarine or butter, room temperature

Preheat the oven to 400°F (205°C). Place the pears in a large bowl; sprinkle with the lemon juice. In a small bowl, combine the sugar, flour, cinnamon, and lemon peel. Sprinkle over the sliced pears, tossing gently to coat. Spoon the pear filling into the pastry shell; set aside.

For the topping, in a medium-size bowl, combine the topping ingredients. Blend with a pastry blender until crumbly. Sprinkle the crumbs over the pears. Bake for 45 minutes or until the pears are tender. Serve warm.

Yield: 8 servings

1 serving contains: *Cal 344kc, Prot 4gm, Fat 11gm, Chol trace, Carb 60gm, Fib 4gm, Sodium 134mg*

Fresh Peach Pie

A mouthwatering summer treat with either peaches or apricots.

Roll out and fit half of dough into a 9-inch pie pan. Preheat the oven to 400°F (205°C). Place the sliced peaches in a large bowl. Drizzle the lemon juice over the peaches and toss gently. In a small bowl, combine 1¼ cups of the sugar, flour, nutmeg, and lemon peel; mix well. Sprinkle over the peaches, tossing gently to coat. Spoon the peaches into the pie shell. Roll out the remaining dough to fit pie. Place over the peaches; make a slit in the top crust. Spread the margarine over the top crust and sprinkle with the remaining ½ teaspoon sugar. Bake for 50 minutes or until brown and bubbling. Serve warm.

Yield: 8 servings

1 serving contains: *Cal 448kc, Prot 5gm, Fat 16gm, Chol trace, Carb 73gm, Fib 3gm, Sodium 132mg*

Dough for a 9-inch double-crust pie, page 302

4   cups fresh peaches, peeled and sliced

2   tablespoons lemon juice

1¼ cups plus ½ teaspoon sugar

½   cup unbleached or all-purpose flour

¼   teaspoon ground nutmeg

1   teaspoon grated lemon peel

½   teaspoon margarine or butter, room temperature

Pineapple-Rhubarb Pie

Blending two distinct flavors creates an unusually good taste.

Dough for a 9-inch double-crust pie, page 302

1½ cups crushed pineapple with juice

1½ cups sugar

1 tablespoon cornstarch

5 tablespoons unbleached or all-purpose flour

3 cups rhubarb, cut in small bite-size pieces

1 teaspoon margarine

Roll out and fit half of the dough in a 9-inch pie pan. Preheat the oven to 450°F (230°C). Drain off ¼ cup juice from the pineapple; set aside for another use. In a small bowl, combine the sugar, cornstarch, and flour; blend well. Place the rhubarb and crushed pineapple in a large bowl. Pour the sugar mixture over the fruit and toss gently to coat well. Spoon the fruit into the pie shell; dot with the margarine. Roll out the remaining dough to fit the pie. Place over the fruit filling; make a slit in the top crust. Bake for 10 minutes; reduce the heat to 375°F (190°C) and bake for 25 minutes longer or until pastry is brown and filling is bubbling. Serve warm.

Yield: 8 servings

1 serving contains: *Cal 451kc, Prot 5gm, Fat 16gm, Chol trace, Carb 74gm, Fib 2gm, Sodium 135mg*

Strawberry-Rhubarb Pie

A perfect springtime dessert.

Roll out and fit half of the dough in a 9-inch pie pan. Preheat the oven to 400°F (205°C). In a large bowl, combine the strawberries and rhubarb. In a small bowl, combine the sugar and cornstarch; sprinkle over the fruit, tossing gently to coat. Spoon the fruit mixture into the pie shell; dot with margarine. Roll out the remaining dough to fit pie. Place over the fruit filling; make a slit in the top crust. Bake for 45 to 50 minutes or until brown and bubbling. Serve warm.

Yield: 8 servings

1 serving contains: *Cal 441kc, Prot 4gm, Fat 16gm, Chol trace, Carb 72gm, Fib 2gm, Sodium 136mg*

Dough for a 9-inch double-crust pie, page 302

2   cups fresh strawberries, cut in quarters

2   cups diced rhubarb

1¹/₂ cups sugar

5   tablespoons cornstarch

1   teaspoon margarine, room temperature

Piecrust with Oil

A nice flaky crust.

2 1/4 cups unbleached or all-purpose flour

1/2 teaspoon salt, optional

1/3 cup very cold skim milk

1/2 cup plus 1 tablespoon canola oil, chilled

Place flour and salt in a large bowl. Combine the milk and oil; pour all at once into the flour. Mix gently with a fork until blended. Divide the dough in half. Place one half between two sheets of wax paper; refrigerate the remaining dough. Gently lift the dough and wax paper; place paper side up in pie pan. Remove the paper, fit the crust into the pan. Repeat with second half of the dough. Leave unbaked for fruit pies and proceed with fruit pie recipe. For a baked crust, prick the crust with a fork. Bake in a 475°F (245°C) oven for 8 to 10 minutes or until golden brown.

Yield: 2 (9-inch) Piecrusts or 16 (3 1/2-inch) servings

1 serving contains: *Cal 134kc, Prot 2gm, Fat 8gm, Chol trace, Carb 14gm, Fib trace, Sodium 64mg*

Lemon Snow Pudding

Wonderfully light and refreshing.

In a medium saucepan, combine the sugar, gelatin, and water. Cook over medium heat, stirring constantly until mixture starts to boil. Remove from the heat and add the lemon juice. Place the pan in a bowl of cold water and cool until the mixture begins to gel. In a large mixing bowl, beat the egg whites until stiff peaks form. Gradually add the gelatin mixture, stirring slowly until blended. Spoon into custard cups; chill until firm. To serve, dust lightly with nutmeg and garnish with lemon slices.

Yield: 6 servings

1 serving contains: *Cal 108kc, Prot 3gm, Fat trace, Chol 0, Carb 26gm, Fib trace, Sodium 20mg*

3/4	cup sugar
1	tablespoon unflavored gelatin
1 1/4	cups water
1/4	cup lemon juice
2	egg whites, stiffly beaten
Ground nutmeg	
3	thin lemon slices, halved

Pineapple Bavarian

So refreshing for a hot summer day.

1 (0.6-ounce) box sugar-free lemon gelatin

2 cups boiling water

1 cup cold water

8 ounces plain reduced-fat yogurt

2 cups crushed pineapple and juice

1 small banana, cut into small cubes

In a medium-size bowl, combine the gelatin and boiling water, stirring until completely dissolved. Stir in the cold water. Refrigerate until the gelatin begins to set. Add the yogurt, beating at medium speed until well blended and fluffy. Fold in the pineapple and banana. Spoon into sherbet glasses or a mold. Refrigerate until set. Serve chilled.

Yield: 12 servings

1 serving contains: *Cal 40kc, Prot 2gm, Fat trace, Chol 1mg, Carb 7gm, Fib trace, Sodium 54mg*

Chocolate Pudding

No special ingredients are required for this old favorite.

In a medium-size saucepan, combine the sugar, cornstarch, and cocoa; stir until the cornstarch is well blended. Slowly stir in the milk until well mixed. Cook over medium heat, stirring constantly until the mixture thickens and boils; boil 1 minute. Remove from the heat. Stir in the margarine and vanilla. Pour into 4 individual serving dishes. Lay a piece of wax paper over each pudding to prevent a film from forming. Serve warm or chilled.

Yield: 4 servings

1 serving contains: *Cal 256kc, Prot 5gm, Fat 5gm, Chol 2mg, Carb 53gm, Fib 0, Sodium 137mg*

$3/4$	cup sugar
$1/4$	cup cornstarch
$1/4$	cup cocoa powder
$2 1/4$	cups skim milk
2	tablespoons margarine
1	teaspoon vanilla extract

Vanilla Pudding

Try serving this with a fruit salad.

2¼ cups skim milk

½ cup plus 1 tablespoon sugar

¼ cup cornstarch

¼ cup egg substitute

1 egg white, slightly beaten

2 tablespoons margarine

1 teaspoon vanilla extract

Pour the milk into a medium-size saucepan; set over medium heat. While the milk is heating, combine the sugar and cornstarch in a small bowl; add the egg substitute and egg white. When the milk is warm, stir about ½ cup of the milk into the sugar mixture, then slowly add that to the remaining milk in the pan. Cook over medium heat, stirring constantly until the mixture thickens and boils; boil for 1 minute. Remove from the heat. Stir in the margarine and vanilla. Pour into 4 individual serving dishes. Lay a piece of wax paper over each pudding to prevent a film from forming. Serve warm or chilled.

Yield: 4 servings

1 serving contains: *Cal 221kc, Prot 7gm, Fat 4gm, Chol 2mg, Carb 41gm, Fib 0, Sodium 176mg*

Pineapple-Cherry Sherbet

John's childhood favorite.

In a large bowl, beat the egg substitute or egg and egg whites with a whisk. Add the evaporated milk, skim milk, sugar, pineapple, cherries, and vanilla. Stir to blend well. Pour into two (2-quart) shallow casseroles. Cover with foil or plastic wrap and place in the freezer until frozen. Let stand at room temperature for 5 minutes before serving. Spoon into dessert dishes. Garnish with mint.

Yield: 19 servings

1 serving contains: *Cal 127kc, Prot 4gm, Fat trace, Chol 2mg, Carb 28gm, Fib 1gm, Sodium 59mg*

1/4	cup egg substitute or 1 egg equivalent
2	egg whites
1	(12-ounce) can evaporated skim milk
4	cups skim milk
1 3/4	cups sugar
1	(20-ounce) can crushed pineapple with juice, packed in own juice
1/2	cup whole maraschino cherries
1	teaspoon vanilla extract

Fresh mint sprigs
for garnish

Spiced Peaches

Make an extra batch to have on hand. Substitute pears for a change.

1/2 cup sugar

1 cup water

1 cinnamon stick

3 whole cloves

4 peaches, peeled,
cut in half

In a large saucepan, combine the sugar, water, cinnamon stick, and cloves. Add the peach halves. Bring the mixture to a gentle boil, reduce the heat to simmer, and cook until tender. Do not stir. Chill before serving.

Yield: 4 servings

Note: Can serve topped with reduced-fat whipped cream or spoon over reduced-fat frozen ice cream if desired

1 serving contains: *Cal 128kc, Prot 1gm, Fat trace, Chol 0, Carb 34gm, Fib 2gm, Sodium 1mg*

Apple Crêpes

A simple, impressive dessert.

Cook the apples in a medium-size saucepan over medium heat until soft. Stir in the sugar and cinnamon; set aside, keeping warm. To serve, spoon about 3 tablespoons cooked apples into the center of each crêpe; fold over one side, then the other. Spoon 1 tablespoon Orange Sauce over each crêpe. Sift a dusting of powdered sugar over each crêpe and serve.

Yield: 6 servings

1 serving contains: *Cal 224kc, Prot 3gm, Fat 1gm, Chol trace, Carb 52gm, Fib 3gm, Sodium 63mg*

5	cooking apples, peeled, sliced, about 5 cups
$1/2$	cup sugar
$1/4$	teaspoon ground cinnamon
6	Dessert Crêpes, page 85
$1/2$	recipe Orange Sauce, page 246
2	tablespoons powdered sugar

Strawberry Crêpes

Colorful for lunch or brunch.

1 quart fresh strawberries, washed, hulled

1/2 cup sugar

1 cup reduced-fat cottage cheese

2 tablespoons plain reduced-fat yogurt

2 packages artificial sweetener

8 Dessert Crêpes, page 85

1/4 recipe Strawberry Sauce, page 247

1 tablespoon powdered sugar

Set aside 8 whole strawberries. Slice the remaining strawberries into a medium-size bowl. Sprinkle with the sugar; set aside. Combine the cottage cheese, yogurt, 1/2 cup strawberries, and artificial sweetener in a blender. Process until smooth; set aside. To serve, spoon about 2 tablespoons strawberry slices in the center of each crêpe. Top with 1 tablespoon of the cottage cheese mixture. Fold the sides of each crêpe over the filling. Pour 1 tablespoon of the Strawberry Sauce over each crêpe. Place 1 teaspoon cottage cheese filling on top. Dust with the powdered sugar. Garnish with 1 whole strawberry on each crêpe. Serve immediately.

Yield: 8 servings

1 serving contains: *Cal 160kc, Prot 7gm, Fat 1gm, Chol 2mg, Carb 33gm, Fib 2gm, Sodium 158mg*

Piña Colada Crêpes

Pineapple and coconut make a tropical delight.

In a small bowl, combine the yogurt, sweetener, coconut flavoring, and allspice. Cover and chill for at least 30 minutes. In a medium-size bowl, combine the cubed kiwi, crushed pineapple, and mandarin oranges. Add the yogurt mixture, stirring gently to blend. To serve, spoon the fruit and yogurt down the center of each crêpe. Fold the sides over. Dust with powdered sugar and garnish with sliced kiwi.

Yield: 8 servings

Variation:

✦ Substitute papaya for mandarin oranges. Use a wedge of papaya with kiwi slices to garnish.

1 serving contains: *Cal 95kc, Prot 4gm, Fat 1gm, Chol 2mg, Carb 18gm, Fib 2gm, Sodium 62mg*

1	(8-ounce) package plain reduced-fat yogurt
1	package artificial sweetener
$1/2$	teaspoon coconut flavoring
$1/8$	teaspoon ground allspice
1	kiwifruit, peeled, cubed
1	(8-ounce) can crushed pineapple, packed in its own juice, drained
1	(11-ounce) can mandarin orange slices, drained
8	Dessert Crêpes, page 85
1	tablespoon powdered sugar
1	kiwifruit, peeled, cut into 8 slices

About the Authors

Brenda J. Shriver grew up in a small town in Tennessee, where she assisted in a family-owned restaurant. After she moved to Ohio, she worked in different restaurants during summer vacations, learning various aspects of food preparation and handling. After marriage to her husband, John A. Shriver Jr., she was delighted to have the time and freedom of her own kitchen to put into practice all she had been taught about cooking. Due to John's career with a major corporation, they have lived in several different areas of the country. In their travels they have learned to love different ethnic foods and Brenda has acquired many new recipes.

Angela Shriver grew up in Phoenix, Arizona. She is married to our son John A. Shriver, III. She earned her bachelor's degree in dietetics from the University of Arizona and served her dietetic internship at United Health Services Hospitals, Inc., in Johnson City, New York.

Index

Index

Index

Index